ISBN 978-1-333-62990-8
PIBN 10528501

This book is a reproduction of an important historical work. Forgotten Books uses
state-of-the-art technology to digitally reconstruct the work, preserving the original format
whilst repairing imperfections present in the aged copy. In rare cases, an imperfection in
the original, such as a blemish or missing page, may be replicated in our edition. We do,
however, repair the vast majority of imperfections successfully; any imperfections that
remain are intentionally left to preserve the state of such historical works.

1 MONTH OF
FREE
READING

at
www.ForgottenBooks.com

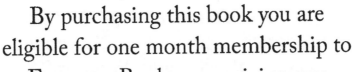

By purchasing this book you are eligible for one month membership to ForgottenBooks.com, giving you unlimited access to our entire collection of over 1,000,000 titles via our web site and mobile apps.

To claim your free month visit:
www.forgottenbooks.com/free528501

ORPHEUS AND EURYDICE.

A GRECIAN TRAGEDY.

PLATO'S VERSION.

By JOHN PENNIE, Jr.

ILLUSTRATED.

ALBANY, N. Y.:
J. B. LYON COMPANY, PRINTERS.
1901.

ILLUSTRATIONS.

INTRODUCTION PREFACE

BY THE AUTHOR

To ORPHEUS AND EURYDICE

A GREEK OPERATIC TRAGEDY

It is not meters, but meter-making argument, that makes a poem.— EMERSON.

BEING fully aware herein, of the height I have attempted to climb, and emboldened by expressed opinions of friends presumed to have competent knowledge of the subject, the following version of the poem " Orpheus and Eurydice " is submitted to the public with some confidence of their approval.

As the Olympic Games have been reproduced at Paris and will be again at Athens and other cities, it seems to prove a trend towards Greek thought in literature — a revival of its drama and fable.

The Death of Orpheus, an epic poem, was written by Homer about the year 900 B. C. Additions were made by Plato 400 B. C., and some supposed errors corrected by Aristotle at request of Alexander the Great, 330 B. C.

An epic poem (defined) should contain a complete subject. Ancient, historical, and descriptive mainly of tragic events, founded on facts — embellished with fiction — should be rendered in suitable language quaintly expressed, harmonious in song, if operatic — should be instructive, philosophic, and moral, with strong probability and natural expression.

Strict rules in composition are pedantic; better with some errors than hypercritically perfect. An epic poem should move the passions and affections with elegant and appropriate thoughts and incidents. The author takes the liberty of inserting his own comments and probabilities as to the real and fabulous parts therein. The hypercritic muse may insist the measure be exact — yet knows repeated couplets tire the ear and detract from nature's common sense.

The author, notwithstanding what others have written, ventures and submits this, his version of what Plato is supposed to have said in repeating this ancient story of Orpheus and Eurydice, which he is presumed to narrate before the assembled scholars at the Odeum — the great theater near the Parthenon at Athens. Likewise with some additions, amendments, and comments in some degree therein connected, including The Argonautic Expedition, The Delian Festival, The Olympic Games, The Demise of Eurydice, the Bacchanalian Feast, and The Death of Orpheus.

From the following historical record, " Orpheus of Thrace was historian of the Voyage of the Argo — successor of Apollo, received from him the harp and lyre as poet, bard, and orator. Upon the Argo's return he was to marry Eurydice; but upon the day, as the tale was told, she died by the sting of a serpent — in point of fact, caused by excess of joy upon seeing him crowned by the Judges at the Olympic Arena. His sorrow thereby caused him apparently to slight and look with contempt upon the women of Thrace, who, in revenge, tore him to pieces under the excitement of a Bacchanalian Revel."

" The Death of Orpheus " has been put on canvas, and is one of the most celebrated masterpieces of

French art. It was painted by Emil Levy, at Paris, in 1878. It has been engraved by Goupil & Co., and published with other superb French and German masterpieces of two volumes each by Gebbie & Co., of Philadelphia, Pa., copyrighted. Inserted herein by permission. The painting is in the Luxemburg Gallery, Paris.

The author gives thanks to David McKay, Esq., publisher of " Bulfinch's Age of Fable and Beauties of Mythology," revised by the Rev. J. L. Scott, D. D., of Philadelphia, Pa. (a most excellent work), for permission to use herein some of its illustrations.

To a certain extent chronological data is ignored herein. Historical incidents in the Heroic Age of Greece, even to the fifth century B. C., are unreliable. The poets have made the same (true or false) highly interesting, classic, and delightful.

The author ventures without fear, as " Jason of the Argo " and his compeers, an attempt to capture, if not a " Golden fleece." He hopes to give at least some pleasure to those who may read this Grecian story reproduced, with a more plausible history in an entire new dress.

Fable elucidations bear pleasing explanations; they are the ornaments used by the poets. The mythological are thus understood.

JOHN PENNIE, Jr

The following gratifying indorsements of friends are published by consent.

J. P., Jr.

" University of Illinois,

" President's Office.

" My Dear Mr. Pennie :

"*I have read your version of Homer's poem, 'Orpheus and Eurydice,' through with great pleasure and continued interest.*

"*The fascinating story has been reproduced by you in a way to interest the casual reader and man of affairs.* * * *

"*I cannot refrain from expressing surprise that you are able to apply your mind to such highly exacting literary effort.*

"*With best regards, I am sincerely yours,*

"ANDREW S. DRAPER."

"Albany, N. Y., *May* 3, 1891.

" My Dear Mr. Pennie :

"*I listened with great interest to the reading of your version of Homer's poem, 'Orpheus and Eurydice,' wondering all the time how it was possible that one who has given his whole life to mercantile pursuits could find time and pleasure in this occupatiou, displaying mental activities and labors creditable to known literary men and scholars.*

"*I congratulate you upon the possession of powers I had not anticipated.*

"*With great regard, your friend,*

'MAURICE E. VIELE."

"Albany, N. Y., *May*, 1901.

" Mr. John Pennie :

" Dear Sir.— *Having read your version of Homer's epic poem, 'Orpheus and Eurydice,' and being familiar with Greek literature, with its theology, etc., I commend your admirable production. It is both pleasing, natural, comprehensive and complete.*

"*The story is told by you as being delivered by Plato before the students at Athens in presence of Socrates. This is cleverly brought about and is somewhat new in literature.*

"*The explanatory remarks introduced by you at different stages of the poem, give it animation, connection and historic interest.*

"*It is an art production of considerable merit. It is Grecian thought in action and tragedy, such as Plato in part might use and recite before the scholars at the Lyceum, as set forth by you, I pronounce it highly tragic, dramatic, musical and poetic, enlivened, likewise, with comedy of a high order. I believe it will, if published, be highly appreciated upon its literary merits.*

"*Yours very truly,*

"P. J. WALLACE."

INSCRIBED

WITH PARENTAL AFFECTION

TO

JOHN C. PENNIE

WASHINGTON, D. C.

OF UNION "K. A." CLASS '77.

GOTTINGEN, '79.

BRESLAU. 1880.

(xi)

AURORA (RENI).

GRECIAN TRAGEDY

ORPHEUS AND EURYDICE

At Athens, as announced, Plato* appears before
the audience in the Great Hall, the Odeum, to repeat
the Homeric story of Orpheus and Eurydice, Socrates
presiding, who, as a prelude, said:

"The Argonauts dispersed the pirates of the Eux-
ine, and to commerce opened the Danube's mouths;
Orpheus as diplomat, poet, and historian, upon his re-
turn, relates the adventures of the Argo and its suc-
cessful voyage before the multitude and judges at the
Olympic games and won the olive crown."

Plato had a full audience as he stood before the
Athenian scholars, and, in easy, flowing measure,
said: "Orpheus, famed of old, admired of Apollo.
The sweet singer, having received the lyre from
his hand as his most worthy successor, whose touch

---

* Plato, a most illustrious philosopher of antiquity, died at
Athens, 348 B. C., age 81. His language beautiful and correct,
and his philosophy sublime.

produced such harmony with song and voice attuned, that the animate and inanimate of earth, the very rocks and verdure of the fields, the woods and birds therein, delighted moved or silent was, listening to sweeter, more attractive songs than theirs, with a flow of melody more continuous; so that the wild became tame, approached, and fain would leave their native haunts to domesticate with him.

His music, voice and song detained Diana's Nymphs when on their way to worship at the Temple of Delos, causing them to halt, to leave the chase, and her of whom we speak was captive made, and broke her vow, alas! as a novice of Diana's.

'Tis said Orpheus' music was so divine to the ear that Hermes could but approve Apollo's choice in him. Luna nightly shone more bright when with his harp he sang. The Muses acquiesced, conceding that such rendition held the key to the heart, sciences and affections, and was irresistible. Calliope, his mother, viewing from the Shades, joyed that her early teachings were not in vain. But alas! as sounds, those with sweetest voices cease to speak, the heart and harp hath a broken string. He died — was slain.

The tale will many a repetition bear. Ages have passed since then, but Grecian maidens still adore him, when e'er they hear his name or speak of love, and sigh, and say, 'we know not such an other!'

The Muses weep for such as he (the pure of earth) there are so few.

They buried him on Mount Olympus, near Heaven his place of birth, and in soothing plaint, Philomela sings above, as if to call him back again.

The zephyrs, sweep with joy through the vale, to join the echo of his anthem, sung on Mount Olympus, where Juno in beauty reigns and Jupiter presides.

Orpheus' music is still heard therein (the resort of the
Gods). There Venus, Love and Hymen come, to rest
in its shady walks. There had Orpheus played and
sang his sonnets — his mystical hymns to the Gods.
Hymns now held sacred : there, at first, Eurydice met
him — ' Dawn of brightness ! ' attracted thither, not
by sound of harp or lyre, entire — 'twas more, 'twas
early love. Its discovery gave mutual joy, tho' should
its flame increase the shrine and Diana will be of-
fended — the sisterhood of Delos be shock'd.

But Orpheus' life and death will tell us what of
music, what of love — their power and possibilities,
that mortals may perceive and admit the divine
therein, and adore the first great cause thereof; be-
lieve, and feel that all his works and laws are highest
harmony, sweetest music, purest love, displayed on
earth to prepare us for Elysium. Such belief should
soothe sorrow's wounds, give valor to the sons of Mars,
and cause the tongue to praise, and with eloquence to
flow. Music rendered by Orpheus did awake the old
heroes, and recall the wild music of the onset; that
they would again shout their defiant cry of victory.
What, tho' later came, alas! music's voice in the
measured tread — the muffled drum, the requiem and
dirge.

This recognition of valor, tho' rendered late, will
ever be a solemn offering, that the Gods may accept;
such, contented die, as wounded, they listen to the
martial airs — the music and the valor told in the old
songs of his native land.

Such heroes — such sacrifices great Zeus will not
despise. In brief, thus sang Orpheus before the poets
and Grecian warriors at the Olympic games ; and thus
obtained his fame, as successor of Apollo in music,
song and eloquence (terms synonymous) so said they,

the Judges, as they the olive crown awarded; so said they who bore him off triumphant, mid shouts and loud acclaims.

That envied prize obtained was the climax of his prosperity — the Muses' halo — the brow encircled poet's fame — won, with smiles and words of praise that the ambitious seek, and friends and loving hearts give, extol and venerate.

Effort to excel, pervade the strong of soul — for fame, for right and nation. Orpheus strove for these, but not for fame alone. He had returned to Athens for love, to claim that, that is admitted to be, the most agreeable delight to man — the possession of a loving and beloved object; such was to him Eurydice.

He had, with eye and ear, inhaled the music of the spheres: — those discernings were hereditary, his; to him they pervade all nature in the germ, in the bud and blossom, in the spring winds piping through the reeds, in the gurgling of the waters from fen and creek, by the way, loitering, lapping wave on wave, that kiss each other and purer pursue their travel to the broad waters, whose splash and spray reveal their light prismatic colors — so, in the grand, boundless billows of the ocean, in the storm and calm, in the gentle rain and in the torrent, in the warm and glorious sun, and 'neath the placid moon, in their light and shade, that tinge and illume the mountains and the valleys. They were to him more glorious, more sacred than all the man-carved gods of deluded worshipers. They have no terror, for they delight, they adorn the earth, and in their never-ending change give happiness to man. Roar Boreas, the earth's extremes are thine; drive the clouds, tear the sail, or with gentle sweep blush the ripening grain. Come Neptune! with thy white mountains crowd thy way to the currents that flow beneath; carry thy frozen bulk to warmer waters, and take the finny shoals refreshment, the walrus and the seal will not complain — monsters of the deep, throw aloft thy spray of brine, from depths unfathom'd brought — sing, birds of every zone; feather'd friends, come, sip from bounteous Nature's store; and fiercer creatures (that provide for thine own with much solicitude) come, eat and slake thy thoats and live. Bright orbs, with thy wandering or fixed light, beyond the blue, that were guides of the Argo, rejoice, twinkle thy delight, shine and speak thy praises to Nature's God — his music of the spheres — his harmony sublime and love divine.

No stranger was Orpheus to the parts therein — he knew each bud and blossom, their seed and harvest time; he knew the birds that come and go — the seagulls, the swift of wing, and the twitterers, their calls and carols, whistles and cooings; for, in imitation, if he but called or sang, they seemed to know his voice, and fearless came; where e'er he moved they followed, nearer came to listen and to wonder, so that the woods were all in motion with charmed appreciation; some, in joy, essayed to wreath in circles with expanded wings above his head, as tho' in act awarding in mimicry a crown, such as the judges give at the Olympic games to the victorious. Eurydice once (a happy time) plaited such a wreath, with leaves and flowers, aided by other clorises, and in merry frolic crowned him, as tho' foretelling an event — it was before he sailed with Jason on the Argo — and many joyous voices chorally applauded; tho' other maidens, standing by, amazed were — not daring, tho' envying — they felt that she was in possession; that Orpheus' heart was hers; that she held the will of him she loved. The maidens kindly smiled and congratulations whispered — could he not indite the choruses (the mystic hymns), render the oratorios of Apollo, and the senses charm to acquiescence, and love invite.

But now, maidens, novices and friends were preparing for the Delian feast, for a journey to Delos, and little Terpsichores came, like dancing skiffs, with fruits and flowers, from many a garden and cove put out, to the Great Barge, to join the goodly throng. The soft music, perfume of flowers and gaudy colors did show that not a fear or cloud was near, as they, towards Delos departed from the Piræus.

The Olympiad more than half its time had sped, since the sailing of the Argo.

To be in reserve, and to escape importunities, Eurydice now lingered long at the shrine of Diana, until with her nymphs her name had been enrolled, but sighs and anxious thoughts would come — an orphan, no mother in whom to confide. * * * The serious, who contemplate the changes and frailties of life, its feeling, joys, have intuition of superior things, more perfect than those of earth — she thought to find them at Diana's shrine, and at first was noted, apt, impressive, and as most devout. But she ever thought of him upon the sea, even when in the midst thereof it would intrude.

Oh! that he had not been away! In her heart love had been pleading — throbbing all the day — mingling with each thought, until at night love sang soft and low to Venus:

To Venus:
Tune: "Henry has gone to the wars."
All my joys, with my lover, are gone;
His absence has saddened my face,
But I bade him seek fame and begone
To be victor, and first in the race.

I was pleased that so fondly he said
    " I sail on the Argo for Fame
But, when I return, we will wed
    If thy hand and thy heart I may claim."

And Neptune has borne him away
    And they say that he ruleth the sea,
Then why should he not, if I pray,
    Return my heart's treasure to me?

The gardens, the groves and the bowers
    I visit no more to admire;
I care not to gather the flowers,
    For I've lost for their love a desire.

I could not be sad, were he here,
    But bird-like would sing in my glee,
For then he would still every fear
    And bring his love-promise to me.

And the promise so truly he gave
    That Jove will keep watch from above
And my hand and my heart he shall have,
    When he comes and he claims me for love.

A perfect calm is irksome; to be awake and con-
scious is better than dull sleep. The morrow came
and went and came again. A bird that would be free
and with its mate, would force the wicket-gate or any
other cage, and flee away, to aid and build with him
a pendant nest in the woods, and there sing to him
in love and be content!

The routine before the shrine — the march and
countermarch, adorations, prostrations, hymns and
vigils, vain and unavailing. Oh, they were a continued
dull monotony that more irksome grew; 'twas calm,
but such a calm on ocean, no sailor likes; its glassy
surface tires the eye, qualms the senses — to be for-
ever so. He would take the risk, and be in storm;

be his own pilot; trust to Neptune, trust to Jupiter and the good ship.

But she, with her fellow nymphs, were promised recreation on the morrow — she to direct the chase, and they the timid deer will hunt; perchance this languor will depart; if not, it may affect the heart, then, then what? Trust to Diana! They sang a hymn to her in worship :—

Chaste Diana! we adore thee
  For thy wandering mother's sake
That thy father prised her beauty
  And her love didst not forsake —
For Latona's Isle, He careth —
  He her memory doth revere
Guard our shrine, Diana dearest,
  Grant thy blessing to our prayer.

Chaste Diana we adore thee
  In this island-home secure
For scenes serene 'mid quiet sea,
  Where all is peaceful, bright and pure,
  Let the jealous Juno never —
  Nor Venus vain, come ever near,
But let Lavarna steal the quiver
  That Cupid's arrows wound not here.

Light of evening, shine upon us!
  Let thy crescent feature smile,
Luna in heaven — do not forget us;
  Thou art the goddess of our isle.
Let no Paris us discover,
  Let no Dido shed a tear,
Let no once forgotten lover
  Find the virgins sheltered here.

At its close Eurydice's voice trembled — the air was chill, they would retire. Thoughts of the absent, as of the dead, will show its grief and bring a tear:

she turned aside that others might not see she had a
sorrow hidden — a regret. She was but as a bud in
a garden of flowers, when Orpheus went to sea, and
he, younger than Adonis, as full of promise. In much
favor by the princes he was held, and therefore with
them joined he the Argo's crew, to gain a name and
fame, and aid in the capture of the Golden Fleece;
'twould have been folly to object. ' He will return,'
she said, ' but it will not be anon! will it ever be?'
Despondingly she sighed, ' Shall we ever meet again!'

The longest vigil endeth, highest mountain hath
its summit, the deepest sea its shore: the stars will
guide him back again if — if the Fates and Neptune
permit — they will! they must! Words rash and un-
befitting for a novice. Oh, forgive her! With nervous
energy, she exclaimed, ' Jupiter, Great Jupiter, over-
rule them all, let him return!'

She had attended the Delian festival at Delos at
a time when he, Orpheus, was at sea, and was so
charmed with its pillared, marble halls and colonnade,
its shrine of polished parian, its statues, Latona, Diana
and Apollo and other symbols, that call for adoration;
its baths, its shade and sunlit walks fit for a Juno-
Temple, most beautiful, that sat as a pearl amid the
Cyclades, its unstained front reflected in the sea —
whose height seemed so near celestial skies from every
point, encircled in a sapphire ring — a sacred, silent,
cold enchantment, things evil came not near — so
calm, so still, so pure. Only at the Delian festival
was heard songs of merriment; at other times only at
set of sun was heard voices of worshipers that sing
and pray — so spiritual that those who came to look
or gaze were fain to stay, even tho' unprepared to
leave the earth's attractions. Thus lured from the
world, her choice of life not fixed — wavering. 'Twas

thus she entered this choicest of Diana's abodes; mature, domestic minds had won her to remain a novice. ' Her voice,' they said, ' would aid and grace the sacred choir, so innocent so pleading;' thus, their flattery aided to accomplish. Then Orpheus in her thoughts was not — so long at sea — 'he must be lost!' She would remember him with others, when at times, at prayer (if in her heart, kept secret, it will not meet with censure). Then with voice suppress'd she sighed and sang a regret :—

A CONFESSION.

Tune: " So fine this morning early "

" Oh! who can cheer the lonely?
   He comes not, and I wait in vain
For his voice and words, that kindly
   Hath kindled this fond, anxious, pain.
Delights, that seen but with Him
   Are treasured joys that still remain
As, when we sang our evening hymn
   At Diana's sacred fane.

There was no eye so cheery,
   No step so buoyant in the grove,
His smile beamed on me dearly
   With words so full of joy and love —
But I dare not now avow it,
   For that would shame Diana's train,
And my vow would not allow it —
   Ah me! could we but meet again
Then — tho' I might my love repent,
   I would confess and die content.

Pleading to Venus, she leant upon her statue.
   Hear my whisper, Venus — when,
  When will my lover come again.
    Never have I loved another,
    Only Him — I have none other.

Thou with Cupid when at play
Was it sinful, say, I pray
　　To heed his song, to praise the lay
　　And sigh, as I, now he's away.
　　　　Shall we! shall we ever meet again?

Insisting did he snatch a kiss,
Didst feign him nay — with soft resist
　　The flush upon thy cheeks relate
　　Consent. that he might captivate —
So I, the day he sailed away,
Parted with him on the quay,
　　Then he — caress'd me as a child
With heart's consent beguiled.
　　　　Shall we! shall we ever meet again¿

It was a ruddy-featured boy
That caused Latona's double joy.
　　Babes that nestled at her breast
　　Apollo with Diana — blest —
Her prayer was heard by the Supreme,
Lend — lend thy aid, we pray to him,
　　He can forbid and he allow
　　He alone annul my vow.
　　　　Shall we! shall we ever meet again¿

Do but grant these only wishes;
I'll repay thee with caresses.
　　Promise me when on Olympus,
　　Thou wilt bid the Gods to bless us.
Let me not forever weep
As tho' he lay 'neath ocean deep.
　　My love, my secret wishes keep,
　　Let me kiss him in my sleep.
　　　　If! If we cannot meet again!

" Let him the billows safely cross and guide him to
Delos ; of him I dream, for him I weep, hear his voice
and kiss him in my sleep. He'll come! He'll come!
I know he'll come, and the Argo will return!" She

believes the purport of her prayer — no more forlorn.
Oh, joyous hope! now the weary time flies by —
beauty smiles again, the lengthened face is more
rotund.

Buds blossom and decay, their bright leaves fade
away, so doth a maiden's sigh; she is now merry with
Diana's nymphs, preparing for the chase, singing of :—

"HUNTING THE DEER."

Nymphs of Diana, haste and away
To join the chase at break of day.
   The horn will echo, hounds appear
   On mountain range to start the deer.
     Ye O! we call! Ye O, steady!

Alert was he, at bay of hound,
And swiftly sped he o'er the ground.
   The doe, o'er mountain 'scaped away,
   The stag had lead the hounds astray.
     Ye O! we call! Ye O, steady!

So startled were they, as he went,
No speeding arrow had been sent —
   No pouch of game, but 'bide the loss
   We'll yet make merry, at Delos.
     Ye O! we call! Ye O, steady!

He swam the lake, and fled away,
And foiled were they — he won the day —
   As if defying them to take
   His antlers, wave, above the lake.
     Ye O! we call! Ye O, steady!

The hounds return, with panting breath;
The lake was deep, to sink was death.
   Diana's troop, with buskin'd feet,
   Had, all with dew, their jerkets wet.
     We sigh, heigh-ho! ye O; heigh O!

The youth is now a man. The weary time at length is past for the Argo's crew. They have returned and there is great joy at Athens, and the faithful dames and maidens fair are there, and met them at the landing with many a caress. Eurydice was absent and Orpheus was sad, but when the truth was told his joy returned and he is safe in port. He knew the retreats of the deer and the resort of the fair hunters — their grounds and woods; for these (for them) had been by special use and law provided. Delos was but a few leagues or so away. Orpheus would fain have sought permission, it would not have been denied, but he rather chose to wander to its mountain heights without, and at leisure view the scenery and towers of Delos.

But what knew Eurydice of the Argo and its return? Oh, it was night, that from her dormitory she by the stars' light saw the Argo pass, returning to Athens, and a bird, her heart, fluttered in its cage. ' 'Tis he! 'tis he!' she exclaimed, ' I know the pennant that I made for Jason ' (his dear friend).

They passed as near the sacred isle as permission gave. Orpheus flush'd his kerchief toward the beacon-light; he knew not who kept vigil. The sailors were joyous, singing hymns to Neptune, that all sailors sing, as in safety they return.

When it passed and her eyes its sails no more could see — as a child that knew its mother near, she closed her eyes and slept and had a happy dream of him — that they would meet again.

Orpheus had met with many greetings, and of absent friends had been apprised, and mindful of them he chose at times to climb the mountain heights to better view the constellations, taught by Urania, and note their fixity — perceive the earth move and the

subordinate moon follow. But such a constellation as
Diana's nymphs returning from the chase he never
among the stars so much of beauty saw. They saw
him, but did not fly, but nearer many paces came, to
better hear the harp and song. He sang to Venus
Urania. They knew the air but not the words — they
listened as he sang :—

TO A STAR.

Tune: " Isle of beauty."

Stella beauty, far above me,
Brilliant orb! within the blue.
Frown not, if an earthly beauty
Dares eclipse thy distant view.
Venus Urania! bright thou art
The eye to cheer, but not the heart.
She comes this way, with hound and horn,
Thou barest no comparison.
Phoebus but shines upon Diana
Coldly — unlike loves glow in man!
The tired nymphs were on their way
To the stony cove, the little bay,
When he accosted her, who lead,
That caused a halt, and gently said:
Fair star of day — hie not away.
Let not a shrine immure thee!
Her fellow nymphs said, timidly,
He speaks to thee, Eurydice.
Her name he now might mention
She expectant — all attention —
Then as they awaited, he ejaculated:
" Illume this sphere — on earth, be dear
Am I not thine — Eurydice! "
Startled, in blush of love she said:
" Orpheus, thy name and fame is known,
Thy songs — I sing — when I'm alone —
Dost thou sincerely proffer love
And plead with me its truth to prove."
And he, without delay, replied,

I do — I love! I woo thee — stay.
I will protect — abide with me.
To Athens let us haste away,
And thou shalt name thy bridal day!
He paused — and she was silent now,
Thinking of her novice vow.
Then said — my home, I leave, for thine
To thee betroth this heart of mine —
(Chaste Delia at Apollo's side
Would happier be were she a bride).
Happy are we, when we are loved;
Woman's heart with love is moved,
But sadder creature never breathed
Deceived by man she once believed.
Clasped were their hands, he kissed her face,
A pledge, responsive, fond embrace —
Then, bade her tell him of the chase,
And when and where the deer had ran.
And she, with rosy blush, began
Her story of the hunt.
"We early sought the woodland shore
With our light barge
And row'd along with muffled oar
To obey our charge.
We landed at the stony cove,
With muzzled dogs in silence move;
Then to the mountains sped along
To circumvent the deer.
They were elate, as warned by fate
And tremulous with fear.
There were but two — they came to drink,
Apparently, together.
He led the hounds to the water's brink;
They quite neglected her.
He seemed to stand as undismayed
When she made her escape.
For then, erect his antlers waved
With confidence elate,
And like a valiant man he stood,
Cared not for barkings hollow,
But walked into the foaming flood

And dared the dogs to follow.
And in they ran, and swam and leap'd
Much in each other's way
Breathless his challenge to accept;
But they lost, he won the day.
He drowned the foremost with his horns,
And broke another's leg.
Now she, I hope, is with her fauns
Afar from any dread!
Their splash and splurge, we dared not follow.
Then, as we came along,
We heard — they, thought it was Apollo
When we heard thy song,
Sang to a queen above our sphere
An imaginary, she —
Then to myself I said, more dear
I could, I * * * I do, love thee! "
And, had he never loved till now.
He felt the twang of Cupid's bow
And fondly, said:
" Dearest, thy maids are in alarm;
They call, they wind their hunting horn
The chase is o'er — bid them depart
And tell that thou hast snared a hart —
Now fear not — pledged to leave Delos
Diana will forgive her loss."
Then, as she unclasped her hound
That lap'd her feet upon the ground
Whined, and would have follow'd,
But she forbade, and it obeyed.
And bounded to its fellows.
One sobbing sylph — unlike the rest
Clung to her neck and was caress'd
Their parting kiss had much of pain
As those who ne'er would meet again
Farewell she said to those on shore,
And lead Diana's train no more.
Then gayly through the woods they wend
To her bridal-mother-friend Penelope

Diana's nymphs, tho' delayed by man's voice —
tho' environed and forbidden, found that his was far
from harsh, 'twas joyous, 'twas agreeable — that they
did linger and backward look; it check'd some merry
voices, and Nature, thawing, made them sigh and
would they were, Eurydice.

Time would not halt; they must away, impatient
they became, 'twas day. To the shrine, they must re-
cross the Ægean to Delos. Some, to the Barge, in
trepidation ran, to return without Eurydice.

The Preceptress was offended, indignant was, and
frowned upon them all, and numerous inquiries made,
and punishment to him who e'er it was, essayed, for
this sacrilegious raid.

Eurydice, at Athens, was fondly received by her
former companions, 'tho some, ominously shook their
heads, trouble foreboding, wondering what would be
the outcome, of this, before unheard of flight, and
desecration of Diana's shrine.

What would the aged priestess and preceptors do,
to punish her. Never were the timid and superstitious
so alarmed; those of questionable age, who never
had been tempted, were shock'd, for so they said —
again and again!

The Archon of Delos was prompt to follow, and
to punish the violators of Religion, and its sanctity
maintain, and thus it came about, for He, with numer-
ous assistants, with their staves of office, proceeded to
the Piræus in force, where lay at anchor the good ship
Argo, and Jason answer'd to the hail of the Archon's
pompous call, 'What would thou, of the cap-
tain or crew of the Argo?' To which he made
reply — 'We seek one Orpheus, to presently and
promptly make answer to the preceptors of Delos,
who, by them, is charged with sacrilege — of violation

and piracy in carrying away one of the novices of the
Shrine of Diana, from where they were in the state
grounds (as is their custom) hunting.' The crew were
instantly on deck, as tho' a squad was in the offing —
and Orpheus was foremost of them all, and promptly
made an answer. 'There is but a moiety of truth in
thy accusations; therefore I, Orpheus, the several
charges therein set forth, deny, and will submit only
to be heard before Athena's Judges, in the highest
court." 'Thou shalt be heard therein,' was the re-
sponse of the Archon. 'But who is here will pledge
for thy appearance.' Upon which the voice of one
rang out, 'Jason, of the 'Argo.'' And the Archon
said: 'It is sufficient. I will so note it down, and so
announce,' adding 'The officials of Delos will lay their
charges home, which, if proven, remember, the penalty
is Banishment or Death!" The sailors, in derision,
laughed, Ha, Ha, a ha, ha! and the Archon and his
aids returned to Athens without a prisoner.

The time was named, that on the third day follow-
ing, at early dawn, Orpheus should appear and an-
swer make in open court, before the Areopagites.

There were but few, who knew of her retreat, the
secret was imposed, and kept; its necessity was evi-
dent. Penelope sheltered her from danger as fondly
as a mother; she had promised to deck her for the
marriage, should she gain permission to wed. It was
noised about, on every tongue, 'Is she in hiding?'
'what has become of her?' 'He must produce her!'

And now, all Athens was astir. The day and hour
arrived, a press of people, wending their way up Mars
Hill to hear the charges laid. The many believed that
sacrilege had been committed; they clamor'd of Diana
— of broken vows, of chastity and punishment.

Trial of Orpheus Before the Areopagites.

The Judges were assembled around a broad circle, on their stone benches seated, in stately vestments toged, their forms and faces mark'd with age and wisdom. Such that silence doth command.

A hum of voices at the great entrance announced the arrival of the accusers from Delos, and other witnesses — novices and preceptors, in their sacristan garments robed. They bore calamitous expressions on their stern faces; they entered, and with their scribes and Archon, stood forth, whereupon the Judges from their seats arose, and paid them deference, as representatives of the Shrine of Diana — and again were seated.

Another, louder hum of voices then arose, and Jason and his swarthy crew jostled through the crowd, but not till they had entered did they doff their caps. And Jason and Orpheus stood conspicuous before the court. The gap in the crowd was closed. The spacious temple could contain no more. The young and old alike, pressing to be nearest, to note and hear and see the participants. The Auditorium, at its center, was occupied by Minerva's statue (said to have been cloven from out the brain of Jupiter). She, of Justice and Wisdom symbolic.

The Judge, who wore the chaplets of the Law, arose, and acclaimed in formal solemnity, as tho' addressing Minerva's self:

"Thou, who art reverenced by the states, and all the Hellenes, wheresoe'er they dwell, and by whose wisdom we preside, we invoke thy aid. Do thou upon the deliberations of thy servants direct and guide us to a just decision, from the evidence to be adduced. That we, the sacredness of the laws hereby involved, may honor and maintain. To hear the charges, to explain and define the Law. Likewise, to hear the defense. The pleas, excuses or reasons that may be advanced and offered to remove the obloquy — namely, the charge of sacrilege.

"'The desecration of the Temple and Shrine of Diana,' that has been (according to report) so strangely violated in the capture and detention of a Novice of Her Shrine — a most serious charge! The accusers may proceed." Whereupon a Priestess of Delos read aloud the charges inscribed upon her parchment-roll, saying, "Reverend Judges, and in Minerva's presence, we affirm, as guardians of sanctity and religion: By the most ancient laws of Greece, established at our Island Shrine of Latona, dedicated by the will of Jupiter to Apollo and Diana, where wisdom, and Religion, health and recreation are dispensed and practised, and Virtue held most sacred — Diana be it known, being acknowledged patron and 'Goddess of the Chase.' The state hath set apart grounds for her Nymphs, only — where man, except by great favor is permitted not, so sacred is it held, undisturbed by intrusion of the lude, and rude, world. We proclaim its sanctity has been violated. We charge, that upon a certain night, for it was not yet day, the accused * * *.'" The Judge arose and said: 'Let the accused stand forth,' and Orpheus, with manly stride, nearer to the symbol of Minerva came, and the matron proceeded. 'That upon the day, as charged, just as Aurora lit the mountain tops, and the Nymphs were returning, tired from the chase, he Orpheus with evil intent, was within the sacred inclosure — did intercept and detain, with music, voice and song — and did, with such persuasive and seducing words and promises, take from the affrighted group, Eurydice, who was, and is, a Novitiate of Diana's Sacred Shrine, therein law and religion scorning. He hath, in defiance of law, Piracy and Sacrilege committed. Therefore, we are in shame before Minerva's Judges, and pray, ask and demand that he be adjudged guilty, and such punishment as the enormity of the offense demands, be meted out upon his head and fortune!'

The matron's voice had reached so high a pitch she was compelled to close the harangue.

The Judge hereupon remarked. 'The accusations have been laid — appear complete. The novice being present, let her be unveiled. Penelope, from a screen, led the maiden to Orpheus' side, where he, with bold and sudden twitch (without an hinderance) threw her peplos off, and the gaze of a thousand eyes were upon her. The judges and all, breathless were, a while, in admiration, gazing — Penelope had adorned her person for the ordeal.

Her long seclusion from the sun's rays had made her very fair; at length the Judge the silence broke, saying, 'Is this the novice?' The preceptress made response — 'It is!' Then (as before some idol) Eurydice bent the knee, and to Orpheus' face looked up; their eyes met, and he, as much as he did dare, caressed her with hand upon her forehead. She in confidence arose, and leant upon his arm. Penelope came to her relief saying, 'I am to be her Thal-ame-polos; in my charge he did leave her.' Orpheus stept aside as the Judge continued, saying 'Is she further recognized,' and many nodded their reply to her identity. Then, addressing the preceptress, he queried — 'The novices of Delos are of various ages — what is a novitiate's full term, e're the final vow is taken, and they are seen no more by man?' To which she made reply, 'The years are five.' 'Was her name, with

her consent, inscribed upon the record?' and the reply followed, 'It has been done.' The matron spoke no more.

There was a pause, until the Judge exclaimed, 'The evidence against the accused is complete — let him now make answer!'

Then Orpheus, with slight tremor, confronting Minerva's Image (the symbol of Justice), said: 'Reverend judges, sacred to me has ever been the Laws of Athena — full confidence have I in the wisdom and decisions of the Areopagus — diplomats from distant lands, quote, and take record thereof, noting their import, and are pleased to adopt such as are passed upon by This Tribunal. Here truth and equity are justly defined — such as relate to property, priority of claims, sacredness of promises (such as are moral, within the law). Those, I affirm, I have not broken. Promises, in good faith received, cannot be broken except by mutual consent! — they are as sacred as religion; for such Religion doth teach and inculcate. The Law doth justly provide rewards for the worthy, who keep their fealty! The barbarian doth honor those who keep inviolate their promises; punishment is only rendered to those who faithless prove.

Thou wilt, therefore, regardless of the favor of the opulent, or power of officials, of shrines or Temples, concede them only such consideration as justice and The Laws direct, and, tho' they be in numbers present, and clamor much, and I be alone in seeming opposition, so pass upon Orpheus, to whom permission has been given to address the court, to speak, and his cause and claim present — I have no fear, by thy decisions, by thy fiat, will I abide.

" Honors, at Athens, are conceded to the aged; for their wisdom, the aged and sedate receive our rever-

•

ence. They have passed passion's violence, and youthful bounds of folly; but Joy, in excess, Great Jupiter in Nature, put in possession of the young, for them. Love's buds unfold — the birds couple, build their nests — creatures then select their mates, 'tis Nature's development of Love. I was not an exception — I as the birds in youth sang; she to whom I sang, with some delight, listened. Each beauteous bud opens its bosom, when Aurora lights Loves garden, and responds with perfume — its vernal tints take deeper hues, that doth reflect its joy thereat, and we behold; such joy I partook of, for more was promised when the flower should its full bosom open. The stately stepping steed will, as it bounds at liberty, arrest its speed, and whinner for its mate. If such is Nature in the lower creatures, who will assert that to man it has been denied. Judges finite, the Infinite in Nature gave each creature Love's desires. In youth I sang in the sacred Choir, and Nature did attract to me one Doric Maid; we sang in unison together. She did perceive, and fearless came to me and I to her, again and again, implicitly. We did select love-tokens, from the buds of Flora that did speak our passion, and gave replies, and thus did Cupid our loves and thoughts exchange; the flame admitted was, and became a sacred contract."

" Treaties with Nations, by Athena's judges, are ever sacred held. In Venus' courts, the promises of Love are not less sacred. On the voyage of the Argo there were other youths pledged to similar loved ones who, upon return, have fulfilled their obligations! Wherefore should not I, in all honor, my promise, my pledged word, redeem; unjust it would have been had I not made the attempt. I have but taken that which was mine own — willingly, mine only

ORPHEUS AND EURYDICE.
(By permission of D. McKay, Philadelphia, Pa.)

" Upon my return, my pledge, to her at sight, was due. Diana's claim contains proviso in abeyance, binding only at close of her novitiate. Note the time, stated by the Advocate, my claim precedence therefore takes, and cannot be denied.

She was sought by the sacred singers of Delos — for religious and reserve her deportment has ever been; she obeyed their behest during long absence; she was a gentle Sibyl with tripod and its fires; she kept the flame of Love alive to give it back to him who first did kindle it, if he should come again." Eurydice, who had drunk in every word, suddenly, and with nervous fervor (that startled the very judges) said: 'Dear sisterhood! Had he not returned, I would have remained with thee forever!' The matron averted her face — she was repulsed. And Orpheus continued: 'For her care, protection, her health, happiness and sustenance, prepared am I to recompense the providers of Delos; it is within the compass of my ability,' and Orpheus drew her to his side, where her head upon his bosom fell.

" Success to Love! Success to Love!" now the fickle multitude cried out. In vain the Archon waved his mace, silence to command. And many affirmative nods, and exchanged glances, from the now animated faces of the judges, was seen; and all about voices rang out — ' For Orpheus! for Orpheus!' was shouted.

The Judge arose and said, addressing Diana's advocate: 'Thou art at liberty to respond,' but she, with haughty voice, replied, 'After this rude demonstration, it would be folly.' Jason a well-filled pouch displayed, hanging from his belt, apparently to meet the exigence, should it be needed.

Then it was the court became of one accord, for

he who appeared to speak for all, read from the Table
of the Law, saying as he read: 'There is no prohibi-
tion from entering the state grounds of Athens.   Love
is not prohibited therein, if it lead to marriage, and the
flame be mutual.   Promises, tho' unwritten, are bind-
ing; cannot be set aside by subsequent agreement with
another, except by mutual consent of the originals so
bound.   The term of the maiden's novitiate, being in-
complete she was at liberty to abandon her sacred
studies and return to her friends, or she could have
been dismissed for sufficient cause.   Her friends are
not obligated to repay for the care bestowed—it is con-
sidered a gratuity; but, still, they may remunerate the
preceptors of the shrine, if they are generous and wise.
We find no violation of Diana's shrine has been
proven, that can sacrilege be called.   No violence was
used in the capture; for it doth appear he did not carry
away this fair novice to his ship, as a pirate might
have done.   It appears he was content to be led by
her, through a circuitous path to the abode of her
friend, Penelope, where later, doubtless, Hymen will
cement their loves and happiness.   There being no
dissent, it is so decreed.   The charges and complaint
of the worthy matron have not been sustained.   No
law by Orpheus has been either broken or defied,
therefore, no penalty is imposed.   The representatives
of Delos will accept such recompense that Orpheus or
his friends may proffer; the scribe of the court will aid
in its adjustment.'

The judges arose and slowly retired in small
groups, with many a chuckle, apparently contented
with the hearing and decisions; some even rubbed
their hands with glee, as pleased they were, e'en the
stern matron smiled as tho' she could forgive.

Now, her timid fellow friends could not be re-

strained; they crowded towards Eurydice to congratu-
late, and many did insist to kiss her. Penelope led
her forth, and as they retraced their steps down Ares
Hill, and through the garden walks departed, their gar-
rulous tongues and merry laughter brightened all the
flowers. A poor wilted one was she, for tho' grown
to womanly estate, they had to lead her, so overcome
she was with their kindly love. They had, with roses,
made an Arch of Triumph at the door, that later Or-
pheus entered when they were gone. They likewise
fed the Doves, intended as sacrificial offering to Diana
— that she might leave her train, and wed.

Beneath a floral wreath they sat her, and danced
and sang The Epi-thal-a-mi-um.

A MARRIAGE IDYL.

Diana, dear! it doth appear
That one in love is here;
She is both plighted and content
But waiting thy consent
To leave thy train, permission gain,
To wed with him she loves.
Her offering brings, with pinion'd wings,
Two sacrificial doves;
And now, never — not for a man
Will she break her vow again.
　　Dance maidens, dance, for she must win,
　　The Epi-thal-a-mi-um!

Let us beg the aid of Juno — now, maidens!
" Queen Juno, dear, send Iris here,
Thy messenger of cheer —
Let all the Gods know this above
That this is a plea of love;
They'll intercede, we do believe,
With Diana of Delos;
Man was to blame — to blame, of course,
For chaste Diana's loss,

OFFERING DOVES TO DIANA FOR CONSENT TO MARRY.

But now, never — not for a man,
Will she break her vow again.
    Dance maidens, dance, for she must win,
    The Epi-thal-a-mi-um!

We'll appeal to the Goddess of love —
Venus, indeed! did Cupid lead,
With his bow and arrow,
And alack-a-day! hearts, beat in love
With quite a bosom throb
What could she do, he came to woo
And she believed him true —
Man was to blame, and love, of course,
That caused Diana's loss.
But now, never, not for a man
Will she break her vow again.
    Dance maidens, dance, Venus must win
    The Epi-thal-a-mi-um!

APOLLO AND THE MUSES (ROMANO).

Around they danced, they sang and kissed, until
she begged them to desist. The merry creatures did
essay to make it Love's own Gala-day!

    Once more! O, let us beg of Fate to be gracious —
    now maidens!
    "To pay her debt, may they beget
    A little Dryade — or — Oreade,
    Then she, might join Diana's train

To make amends — it may be
He never more will tantalize
Or poach, or capture by surprise
With his alluring lover-voice,
Now Fate has fix'd his choice:
Man was to blame, and fate, of course,
For chaste Diana's loss.
But now, never, not for a man,
Will she break her vow again.
　　Dance maidens, dance, for she must win,
　　The Epi-thal-a-mi-um!

Desist, desist, she cried again; whene'er I hear of
　fate or death, I tremble, shrink and faint thereat.
'Tis well, Fate's Fiat we cannot know,
To cause us mortals fret and woe!

"But see, Penelope beckons us within. Come!
Thanks for thy joyous song, and wishes kind, may
they all prove true. Come to the Feast!"

They ran and skip'd, with nimble feet, and left
the flowery Bower behind. Faithful Penelope never
had so many happy guests before.

JASON'S BANQUET.

And Orpheus and his friends at night were jovial
on the Argo, as Jason spread his sailor Banquet, to
which more than one of the judges found their way,
and Momus and Comus, full of fun, rattled off their
wit at Orpheus' expense, and Tipphis repeated his
banter with a nymph in the garden after the trial.
'Tip' strutted in character, and said ' I was singing a
solo,' and they formed a ring to listen, it turned to be
a duet. I sang

THE DUET IN THE GARDEN.

Oh, who would not rise to the Gods?
They dwell not on earth, but in heaven.
They taste of the sweets that delight
That never to mortals are given.
The Goddesses there WE shall meet
And sip their Ambrosia and Nectar,
And loll in their shady retreat,
Just acting as beauty inspector.
What secrets of bliss they would teach,
And sing on Olympus their mirth —
And Juno — a Venus, give each
Far-away, from the dowdies of earth
The slatterns and dowdies of earth.

The maidens laughed Te-e, Te-e, Ha-ha and Te-e,
and a Vixen Dared reply — with

True! who would not fly to the Gods?
They dwell not on earth, but in heaven.
They would give US all perfumes and sweets
Such as man for devouring are given.
We'll invite mother Juno to meet us
With Narcissus and Paris, to greet us,
And with such as Adonis, by dozens,
We'll take them for lovers and cousins;
And Venus, we know, she will plan
For us a better selection than man,
For they will be constant and true.
And Hymen with love bid adieu.
And we do! as we've a-mind to!
So now — there! conceited bear!

They clap'd their hands and laughed inordinately.
Jason said, 'tell us all about it — what didst thou do,
Tiphys?' And 'Tip' replied. 'I made my escape;
I'm here!' A jolly judge (one well-versed in Cupid's
wiles) remarked. 'She'll not refuse thee. But before

Hymen ties the knot, have all superfluous hair from
thy head removed, and see that her nails are pared.'
And Tiphys joined in the laugh. Epicurus robbed
the larder for the feast.   Jason told how, in passing
the Isles of the Sirens, ' Ulysses determined a fishing
to go, and had he not tied a Gordian knot around him
with a hawser, one sailor less would be found among
the crew.' To which a sober judge replied: ' It was
well thou hadst the hawser!' and the loaded table
shook, and the laugh went round. Tiphys sang his
songs, and the boisterous chorus rang, for Tiletus
tap'd a vintage load of bottles, ere the merriment was
closed. Each took his part, in the Symposiac, round
*   * *.   And the disturbed city of the day resumed
its quiet; many snooded. Maidens, great tears let
fall, as they looked upon Eurydice, as Orpheus told
his love. The married too,— as tho' Eurydice was on
trial, whereas, she had not been disturbed by any one
— she had been as a guest at the home of Penelope."
(In repeating the incidents, Plato remarked, ' So ran
the record of the court, and modern Law has not re-
versed Love's obligations.')

" Orpheus was a Prince. The Argo's crew were
princes. By those who knew him, he was much be-
loved. They said of him, ' His soul breathes in his
songs.' With him there was but one choice between
True Love and meritless conceited wealth, that Plato
did express, thus saying, ' Her wealth was in her self,
possessions she had none.'

LOVE OVER WEALTH, SUPREME.

The influential, I opine,
May take a novice from a shrine,
And censures frown may oft escape,
If they a weighty present make.
When done — remonstrance, there is none —

Athena's judges did maintain
That Orpheus had a prior claim —
The law imposed no penalty —
Their love was not impiety.
He, in gold or gems, was one
Would yield them up what e'er the sum
For her alone for that loved one —
Give all of earthly store or cost
And never count such dross a loss.

" Her gentle, unassuming tact will lead; he will follow, love her, in song or sorrow, and she, adore him evermore. Alas! It was too intense! Then, it was fatal, but now, it is immortal."

A LAMENT FOR THE DISAPPOINTED.

Brief are the joys of earth;
They do not satisfy,
So fleeting is the mirth,
So frequent is the sigh —
The dawn of day was bright
But torches lit the night,
For ere the wedding day set in
She died for love of him!

" Love is indestructible; confound it not with other passions. Love is Jupiter's primal trait, endowed on mortals, never to be withdrawn — its full measure is not here, its fruition is (perforce) hereafter; 'twill make amends for disappointments, past, in continuous overflow — good souls! in this assurance, be of good cheer!

" Discordant creatures there are, that roar, snarl and tear, with carnivorous teeth-envying; they spring from the jungle, creep from their lair in ambush, waiting, the innocent to entrap, and fatal is their venom.

The Poets say, that by sting of serpent, died Eury-
dice. Sting of serpent is but a figure of speech for
natural death. Death is a supposed enemy; we do
not desire to die, we would live forever. Fellow stu-
dents, we so understand it." At which there was a
murmur of dissent at the words 'figure of speech;' it
came from the Orthodox in sanctimonious garb —
representatives of Gods innumerable. They were
there, seeking pretexts for censure.

The students, to applaud began, but Socrates pre-
siding, with gavel's call, suppressed the applause.

Such was explanatory — the preface to much of
Plato's lecture. The serenity of his mind was undis-
turbed, and he continued. "Orpheus had returned
with the victorious Argonauts in time to enter the
lists, and strive for the prizes at the Olympic games.
By general consent, at Athens, he had been selected
to relate the adventures of the Argo, and the ship dedi-
cated to Neptune, Father of waters — Ocean's God!"

"There he, extempore orating, melting, thrilling
and intoning with his voice and harp, sang the ex-
ploits and perils of the voyage. The escapes from
Boreas' breezes, flash and crash of storm, battles with
the billows and the clouds, that threatened to engulf.
Hidden rocks and whirling pools, with songs of sirens
met with on the way; furies numerous, and Gorgons
in disguise. But sirens and sea maids their nudity
displayed in vain, for when Orpheus sang of Home,
Dear Home — with that Hymen Enchantment, they
passed the perils and were safe — safe from breakers
and wreckers aloof, steering to deeper waters, safely
sailing. He sang as tho' he were a married man, and
loved the treasures of his home. As tho' addressing
Great Neptune, he sang:—"

OF HOME, DEAR HOME.

Tune: "The Sicilian Hymn."

Would'st thou know why we wander so far from our home?
Dear place! where so lonely they hope we may come,
Those precious, those fond ones, so link'd to our lot,
Have made its retreat the most hallowed spot.
    Home, home! Dear, dear home!
    There's Elysium and bliss with our loved ones at home!

'Twas the care of their welfare, the toil of the day,
That called us, reluctant, from loved ones away.
But oh for its harbor, its shelter from storm,
Where care is excluded, to rest us at home.
    Home, home! Dear, dear home!
    There's Elysium and bliss with our loved ones at home!

There fond arms are open, our pets, how they cling!
And with kisses they hug us tho' nothing we bring;
Our Fates, we accept them, the burdens to come,
For love of our kindred, so faithful at home!
    Home, home! Dear, dear home!
    There's Elysium and bliss with our loved ones at home!

In our voyages, so distant, for them do we sigh,
And in dreamings oft see them as tho' they were nigh;
Their sweet voices greet us, they seem within call,
To share our own confidings, the dearest of all!
    Home, home! Dear, dear home!
    There's Elysium and bliss with our loved ones at home!

We trust we shall see their loved faces again,
In our dwellings contented, all thatched from the rain;
No scene is so tranquil, no cure like its balm,
That in sadness so cheers us as loved ones at home!
    Home, home! Dear, dear home!
    There's Elysium and bliss with our loved ones at home!

There, sorrows are soothed as Angels above;
There are shared our misfortunes with pity and love,
And a joy to our hearts shall its memories be,
Of the dear ones at home, remember at sea.
    Home, Home! Dear, dear home!
    There's Elysium and bliss with our loved ones at home!

Jason called aloud, 'Spread all sail.' At distance mermaids were seen parading in seaweeds, calling ' Ship, ahoy! Ah, there! and say! I say!' ' Epi,' the cook, took it down among his recipes, that later, I may repeat.

During the singing of Orpheus' song, the old sailors hid their faces in their broad, rough palms — the ears of all were listening. Some jacket sleeves were wet, that came not from the salt sea, and, when he ceased his singing, they gazed upon him with strange admiration, as tho' he were a guide, inspired by some blessed spirit, not of this world.

And Hellene's daughters, classic models, from lowest limb in form to beauties famed accepted curve (in proportions eye complete) were at home, awaiting them. And little groups and bevies (companions of the students) smiled, and listened, conscious of Plato's sincerity, pleased with themselves and admired the warm reciter. Plato did not marry, and they wondered why; was it from fear that she would die, and he, like Orpheus, mourn for her?

It was the Nation's greatest holiday. At this Olympiad all the great and petty states of Greece sent forth their delegates and participants. The mentally equipped, the strong of arm, the swift of foot, the equestrian, with his native and Arab steed. The gamester with his dice and tricks, the plausible and the dupe, the simple and the worldly wise. They came, like Egypt's locusts, or as tho' they flock'd to the Judgment foretold by the Prophets. Soothsayers and their oracles, snake charmers, money changers, and dealers in precious baubles. Lavarna with her thieves, and Voluna with her drones, who feed on others' store, that move with the caravan, leaving in their path a blighted trail. Then came the pretentious and the

pious, who came on pilgrimage to forgotten shrines —
sacred to the antiquated, valueless except for lucre's
sake. And the bards and scribes (that falsely tell of
wondrous things), and the nondescripts who mock and
trade, and set their stands with ingenious relics for
the credulous to buy. Then came the vicious, the tat-
tered and the better robed, with their retinue of slaves,
filling the roads, the gardens and the groves of Tempe.
And among the motley throng, the bacchanal and
glutton — keen-eyed adventurers, and wealth with its
pageantry and pomp—of either sex—for woman, not
as yet, had been prohibited. They saw it all, and were
not shock'd, but played their parts and won and lost.
Lost, what? Lost the power to blush! They came, as
barbarians, a lawless host, but human still. The
young were carried and dragged; the aged hobbled,
worn and weary, in need of rest and food, and much
commiseration. Yet be at the Olympic games they
would, tho' never to return. And some (the few),
with natures nearer the divine. They came to the
Great Drama where Orpheus carried the most honored
prize away; remember it was long ago, 'twas told in
Homer's day. Then, here stood The Hecatompedon,
ere Phideas built the Parthenon. That multitude are
dead and gone, their dust unurned, and all but
Orpheus and Eurydice forgotten.

" Sol lit this earthly panorama from sea to isle, from
river's brink to mountain top; the valleys and the
groves were full of perfume, beauteous land, luxuri-
ance everywhere — marred only by the unwashed!

The Judges — the Areopagites, in robes arrayed —
were there; they came at early dawn, and invocations
offered to the Gods, the forms observing. Those
nearest in silence bow; 'twas to that indifferent host

non-essential the words Great Jupiter approved, they
heard them not — no reverence paid.

" The multitude nearer drew to the barrier stakes
around the cordage. The Herald, with trumpet blast,
held aloft the lists to follow out the order of the day.
The coarser games, tho' lengthened tediously, were
won and lost in noisy clamor — sport and wounds the
usual casualties. The previous night had been to
thousands sleepless, spent in bacchanalian revel,
senseless song, and antic dance, where Terpsichore,
with grapey breath, cut fingers never seen before, and
the caterers gathered in the harvest. The more gen-
tle, sensitive element were alarmed — took no part.
Those from the Morea and Crete, with Jason's aid,
found asylum within the sanctum's shelter; they
sighed to perceive the degeneracy of man in that as-
sembled horde. The Muse had deserted the Loved
Land since the last Olympic gathering — since the
Argo sailed for Colchis — so short a time it seemed.
The veterans and sedate, the wise and virtuous, were
at bay—were dumb; they would they had not come.
They came to hear Orpheus orate, and tell of the bat-
tles of the Argo — see the games, and observe and
worship at the statue of Olympian Jupiter, with its
costly inwrought gold and gems. They would be
safe, the discreet replied, and together congregate
near the Judges' elevated stand, where strictest order
is maintained, and would, as early as discretion war-
rant, to their homes return; 'twas thus resolved.
This is no place for Eurydice, the betrothed, or the ma-
trons and maidens who had ventured there, crowded
and jostled in this maelstrom of humanity's remnants
— not all such, believe it not, the worthy and the val-
iant were there, mingled in the whirl and surge, with
its Babel-clack of tongues, its scenes obscene, and law-

less enormities. Oh, for a Lycurgus or a Draco, to hold in check this liberty abused! But what will not Orpheus' music do! He had returned—had he not still'd the storms of the Euxine, opened wide the Danube's mouths, and untamed man and beast driven to their lair, croaking and conquered.

"Tradition, from its mystic volume, obscurely tells the Tale in varied phase; compared herewith we fail to find comparison in any lyric song or tragedy — a morn, so happy-bright as That Olympic day, or so sad, so sorrowful an ending.

"Manly Orpheus! his mind at ease, appareled in his best, entered the Arena, and sang his psalm to Jupiter. Its rendition was inimitable, and in form, began by asking guidance of the Muses and favor on the multitude, and sang to Jupiter devoutly.

PSALM TO JUPITER.

Tune: "My Country 'tis of Thee."

With joyful heart and hand we praise our native land;
    Loyal to her!
Her mountain lands are free, our valleys to the sea
Now render praise to thee — great Jupiter!

Athens, our Capital, our voices shall extol,
    Join the applause!
The Areopagus meet and adopt — discuss
Commerce and happiness and righteous laws.

Olympians Jupiter! false gods shall not deter
    One worshiper!
To Thee our prayers we raise, worship and give Thee praise,
For these our happy days — great Jupiter!

This nation's natal day, we all Thy gifts display,
    Awards to her!
Our shouts and happiness, our thankful heart's express;
Us Thou did'st ever bless — great Jupiter!

Father! continue us, in thy remembrance;
  Let naught deter.
'Tho we have wandered far, we all Thy children are,
Now bless us evermore — great Jupiter!

The illiterate and wise alike praised, felt its force
and application. Poets and orators listened and were
amazed, wishing themselves such as he.

Sages tell us that should he ever come from Heaven
again he will be offered as a sacrifice — for evils done
by others — to appease the offended Gods. Is it pos-
sible? Can we be so base to slay him should he
come?

All will be well, soliloquized Peneolope the faithful,
and Media (Jason's wife) acquiesced. They super-
vised the little circle in their charge.

THE OLYMPIC ARENA.

Orpheus, like a second Hercules, stood forth, in
form erect as Apollo's representative and music's
lord. Then, from deafening clang from Pan, with
all his band, in medleys bray, in mimicry grotesque
beat their gongs and blew their brazen-throated
trumps: and for a while hoarse throats were closed
and Orpheus' theme was heralded aloud, and hushed
was all the clamor. His renown was widely known,
from Macedon to mighty Bablyon, from Sicily to Sa-
lem — "The Young Apollo." The theme was then
announced: "The Argonauts' Return; Adventures
and Heroes of the Argo." Like unto Hercules of
great renown, he in fluency of speech gave record of
the glorious voyage, even as his great progenitor
who brought the golden apples from the garden of
the Hesperides, and the hundred-headed dragon slew

that stood on guard — even as he, the Argonauts, stormed the Forts of Colchis, battled and won, with Media's aid, the stolen Golden fleece. And Jason, he avowed, deserved the largest salvage; and rough Jason smiled upon Media at his side, and other delicate cheeks were rippled as Media blushed.

Orpheus in clearest tones, that were intoned and heard afar, recapitulates the incidents — the miracles, the moats, the walls and gates o'erthrown in planting their banner on the citadel. Aloft he held the symbol of the Grecian states, that had waved defiance to the world. There was a pause, for Jason from the Judges' stand proclaimed aloud, " Neptune, great Ocean's king, the Argo we dedicate to thee," and again the trumpet blared aloud, mid shouts of "Great Captain! great ship!" The log and record of the voyage were recorded at the Parthenon at divine Athena's shrine. And Orpheus resumed and drew comparisons of valor with the renowned of Mar's heroes — Codrus, Theseus and Achilles — with Jason the daring — the hero of the Argo. Then the valor of the crew and the incentives that led the way to victory (facts historic); then the constancy of each ally, composed of the people and princes of the states. Nor was Media or the Penelopes at home forgotten. Had they not furnished indispensables for the voyage, cared for children with comforts scant, and offered prayers for them when they were far away! In comparison he named them among the martyrs — the heroines of all time.

Orpheus, with his large blue eyes, by intuition guided, saw among those earthly goddesses his own Eurydice. He knew who in affection, in form, in face and grace excelled all others. His quick ears knew her Doric accent, with its endearing modulation.

No other she possessed such proofs of joy and love;
she was the one bright light to him of earth.

Then gave he the pilot deserved laudation, and
meted out to all full share of glory — the single and
combined actions and successes of his fellows of the
voyage — till kindred, standing there, were by varied
passions moved, from tears to boisterous acclaim —
as tho' each friend named was the one particular and
deserving hero. The part he took himself he men-
tioned last and least, guiding his thoughts and words
with modest truth, such as draw silent admiration
from sage and stoic. Even then and there he had
Eurydice in mind, and she aware for she was there.
Her own beloved, was it not confessed in the roseate
glow that her fellow maidens lack'd?

There is a climax in life's drama that comes but
once — when we love. At that supreme moment, un-
conscious of its decorum and unforbidden, she ran
within the Arena — childlike ran — and bending low
—kiss'd his disengaged hand. Whereupon, ere she
had gained the place from whence she sprang, an-
other and another shout rang out, that echoed in the
air. It was a pæan of praises, unstinted from a mul-
titude.

Those shouts were not for him alone — plighted to
him was she and many knew thereof. It check'd but
did not ruffle his placid brow or mar the theme.
Orpheus but smiles as she retired, in peril, in uxori-
ousness of feeling. * * *

He knew it not — it was a parting, a last kiss. The
Judges, invested with the robes and dignity of sages,
noted not the intrusion.

He had produced again the songs and tunes of
Mars and Neptune, that fires the eye, that rallies war-
riors of renown, and prehistoric heroes lived again —

such themes that nerve the brave; that battle for the
right; such as built the walls of Thebes and Salem,
or flew to the rescue of a nation's rights — freedom,
honor, symbol — earnest as those who plead a right-
eous cause, or defend the oppressed, forward and on-
ward to conquer. They had opened barred gates,
sunk pirates fathoms deep; those cruel fiends who
build their ships with prows like vulture's beaks, with
expanse of wing that outspeed the gull; to swoop upon
their prey. Now safety, peace and plenty follow on
land and sea and they are feared no more. Bellona
ceased her bellowing, envy hid her face, and the fore-
boders and their oracles are silent.

Their patriotic souls were moved to valor as Or-
pheus continued: 'Media shall stand by Jason; have
they not as one circled the earth together? Now may
the Graces — Autumnus, Felicitas and Flora — sit
them down as household gods, in plenteous harvest,
drink from Castilian fountains and feed upon am-
brosia. The fruits of all the earth are ours, and who
shall dare to cause us an alarm? The Driads, the
Graces and the Muses are in harmony with Historia's
record that cannot be effaced!' Here Orpheus
paused, with look upraised, that appealed to a Judge
they saw not, in motionless peroration.

The shouters rent the air with cheers, in praise, in
exaltation — they knew not when to cease! Then
the earthly judges from their seats arose; their wands
upraised and the olive crown presented, placed it on
his brow, his head adorned, and many gracious words
bestowed. The herald then announced aloud: "Or-
pheus, of famed renown, has won the prize, the Olive
Crown."

Minerva's wisdom had been invoked, but Tasita
and Muta were declared added to the Muses.

" Orpheus triumphant — all hail! son of Apollo! all
worthy Orpheus!" pealed in continuous roar that
ceased not till tongues and throats exhausted were;
so beyond control were they, they would have deified
him had not the day and place been sacred to Apollo.

Orpheus' voice and theme were so adjusted, at-
tuned with truth and tenderness, that envy, spleen and
perfidy impotent were 'gainst record of deeds so
worthy — progress, commerce, industry, freedom,

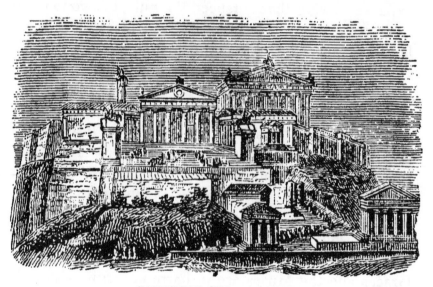

PARTHENON, ETC., AS IT WAS.

wisdom, peace and love! Was not the cargo of the
Argo landed at the foot of the Acropolis? The main-
land and islets of the sea free — free to partake in
equal and deserved share its fruits, its honors and
protection. The grateful and ingrate tolerated — tho'
distant as truth and falsehood — far apart as life and
death with Lethe's stream between.

This was Minerva's boast — Beautiful Athens!
queen of cities, whose glories cannot be hidden —

where the wise do congregate and send their sons, from whom rays of light will shine and Minerva illume the world. Behold her architecture — Doric, spacious, grand and simple; her Ionic, conspicuous, beauteous and enduring, pillared and adorned with statues of the Gods and heroes, explanatory of her history and victories Her temples, parallelogram, similar to the Tabernacle of Moses, intended for religious and similar purposes and the public good!

Twilight tinged the mountain tops with light, but when the pageantry of the day was o'er 'twas as if the sun was in eclipse, and Orpheus was all in all. Have they forgotten — Alas! where was Eurydice? True, the laurel with the olive twined was his, deserved rendition, worth's own most glorious prize. He was to sit on the table of the Judges in the Prytaneum—his place was vacant except some cypress (symbol of sorrow) that there festooned, the seat, it spoke of bereavement, sudden and severe — it was to have been a joyous feast; it was smileless and cheerless. The Judge presiding gave scanty words of welcome, and briefly gave the cause of Orpheus' absence. 'The death of a very dear friend;" few there were that lingered at the feast. Others sought for him, spiritless and downcast. He did not appear in the procession triumphal. Honors and praises were conceded, his name revered, but there unsung. When e'er you visit Altis observe his statue, erected, placed there by those who knew and loved him. * * * Return with me to the time when the prizes were awarded and Orpheus was crowned, the Judges gone; and now the wild youth's pupils of the Muses, in much numbers from the academies, even from Rhodes and more distant lands were there, like untamed colts they bear him off (the victor) in their arms; aloft along like

Phaeton, driving the chariot of Sol; horses unmanageable that set the world on fire, and Proteus of the schools vainly made remonstrance. Bacchus' bowls were filled and filled and emptied; stained were their costly garments with excess of wine, ere the cruse of oil went out. They knew not the torture that they caused; at length (how long he knew not) wearied with their uncouth noise and joy hilarious, Eurebus came to his relief — this prisoner prince escaped, in darkness breaks away, and is with Jason in the free air again. His first and instant thought is now to find her he loves — haply she has long since retired to that asylum prearranged for, ere the day began, obtained within a sacred grove for the maidens and matrons of Athens.

Hastening through the groves to find, they meet a group of women, of Eurydice's fellow-mates, companions of the day, who were returning on the road in search of him. They, in loose ungirdled robes, with countless voices sought to tell him that —that Eurydice was dead! Then, as one dazed by clash and flash from clouds that break the mast, he stood aghast; striving to ravel out their strange and wild exclaimings; at length a matron, "Mother of the sons of Diogorus, he who in excess of joy expired upon hearing that his sons had won prizes (years a gone)," she briefly told the sad, regretful incident; that Penelope suffused in tears (who was to have been her thal-ame-polos at her bridal) confirmed. Trembling he comprehended, he understood it all. " Eurydice had died with excess of joy (so died Sophocles at close of his dramatic victory)." * * * It was at the time when Orpheus was crowned that the cruel Fates (so 'tis said) stung her and she died. They sought to resuscitate the breath and the pulses of her tender

ORPHEUS AWARDED WITH THE OLIVE CROWN — HE IS CARRIED OFF BY THE
STUDENTS — EURYDICE FAINTS WITH EXCESSIVE JOY.
(By Charles Selkirk, Artist, Albany, N. Y.)

heart in vain; no wound was visible. Then, as tho'
he had received a wound as fatal, he fell upon the
earth and gave the first groan and shed the first tear
his brave and harmonious soul had ever uttered. And
other tears were shed by that pitying, mourning
group of friends. Vainly did Jason seek permission
that Orpheus might see her body in the sanctum. The
answer came, " The desire was human but inadmis-
sible, impious to the solemnities of Diana."

With other thoughts, later, at midnight, they were
met to gaze at distance upon her form, as upon a
palanquin beneath a silken canopy she lay, like a
beauteous model for a Phideas chisel, or twin figure
to mate with Athena's in the Parthenon — her para-
gon, in form and feature. War's veterans, unused to
pity, felt his grief; supported Orpheus, at times cov-
ered their emotions with their mantles. Manly cheeks
were wet for him in fellow feeling. Those friends,
sons of Mars and Neptune, led him to their tent, and
sought with wine and words, in their honest, un-
polished way, to bring him to himself again. He
was conscious only of having fallen from Heaven to
earth, powerless before all-potent Pluto. His sting of
death. Eurydice had been carried to the sanctum
of Cybele — she was to be intombed near the shrine
of the Goddess in consecrated ground, whither Or-
pheus knew not. The grounds are at Elis in the
"Elysian Fields" (so called), on the plains of An-
tilata near a Temple and statue of Olympian Jupiter,
and numerous shrines were near. The oracle thereof
refused admission or delay, for insufficient reason
given " That many hours had passed away;' " that
the Olympic games were on," and that " ominous
birds of pestilence had been seen flapping their heavy
wings." The Sisterhood of Novices plaited buds and

flowers that read, " Our grief is painful," and others
that said, " Thy joy be evermore." Penelope was
permitted to lay the garland on the pall at her feet; no
cypress or other profanation. Man, except at dis-
tance, was permitted not to look upon her, claimed
as she was as " Sacred from the shrine of Delos." A
silent symbol of purity, a white rose, was in her hand,
the other as a lily upon her bosom lay. And Orpheus'
frame was greatly agitated. He was held in check by
Jason and his friends — rude interference was impos-
sible; it would have been sacrilege. The warders took
him to an elevation where he could be nearest and
see her face (as there would pass the cortège), but
when it passed he was both overcome with sorrow
and with tears. He was not deceived, he saw her —
her placid, beauteous face, and would have broken
from their charge to intercept, to stay the corse, but
for the compelled restraint of friends and mutes and
guards.

It was between the midnight and the morning hour,
long before the sleepers from their tents are wont to
rise, that the funeral toll began. The torch-bearers
(Galli priests) from the sanctum led the way. The
priestess of the shrine presiding — stately and impera-
tively ordering; warders and mutes silently obeying —
She, in her crescent, mural crown, with her sheaf of
wheat inverted; she with slow and measured step
precedence took, and in loud alto voice proclaimed:

" The pure, the beautiful are Diana's — sacred to
Diana!" Melpomene leading the vestal virgins, in
sandaled feet and faces veiled, and lamps with
flame extinguished; they held the cords and tassels
of the pall under which she lay and others bore the
burden. Nænia's mournful chant was the funeral
dirge. When it began with its wail of woe the sleepy

MIDNIGHT FUNERAL OF EURYDICE.
(By Charles Selkirk, Artist, Albany, N. Y.)

multitude from their tents came out and endless made
the long procession.

Those solemn sounds, at such an hour, caused some
to tremble, but to Orpheus it spoke of hope and Life
Immortal, and passing comfort gave. Again she who
presided intoned: " Maiden thou art sacred to Diana;
her claims are first and last and all supreme!" Vir-
gins replying, "To Diana sacred! Revered and all
supreme."

They slowly pace the way, Nænia singing :—

THE JUDGMENT DAY.

Bless'd day of peace, the promised day,
When pains of earth shall pass away;
Now, love divine, attunes the lay,
They sing in heaven, O joyous day!
    Forgiven, they we'll say.

Cybeles, tintinabula, toll'd between the bars, and
"Sacred to Diana," the response—Nænia singing :—

There, Seraphs with a golden scroll,
Of names recorded will unroll,
And paeans loud will welcome all
Of Jove ordained, who heard the call,
Of Him who loves us all.

Still the tolling bell between the bars was heard,
and "Sacred to Diana; to Diana sacred"—Nænia
singing :—

Oh! happy day, believers say,
Her soul has left behind earth's clay,
To celebrate " The Judgment Day."
Where bliss can never pass away
Like the joys of yesterday.
    Glorious, glorious Destiny!

Cybeles, tintinabula, faintly tolled again, and
ceased with distant voices, " Sacred to Diana; to
Diana sacred."

They had reached the entrance of the encircled wall
and the funeral hymn and chanting cry grew fainter
on the ear as they passed within its fold, where death's
secrets are maintained. She was a novice of Diana's;
it had not been annulled, and 'twas known that none
but the approved and pure may enter there. The
brazen gates are barr'd as the cortège inward pass,
and all without in gloom — in darkness grope, as
they quench their torches and to their tents depart,
with serious thoughts and sighs.

Drooping Orpheus, all piteous, heard its last reced-
ing sound and shed his tears in vain. The earth to
him a desolation was, as Jason led him to his tent —
what now cared he for fame or wreath of bay or
laurel, Eurydice being absent and past recall? He
whose appearance once so brilliant was, now is ob-
livious of himself. The morning broke — Luna hid
her face in seeming clouds of sorrow. Diana in
Heaven, through her Oracle from the shrine, con-
veyed to him its definings: " That immortality was
assured; that he a full fruition should receive of divine
love; that he should higher climb — obey and be satis-
fied. There are many joys they had not known; they
will be reserved till then. Cannot he who gave us
senses fit for earth's necessities give us others for de-
light in Heaven? Kindred souls in joy will meet
again." The Oracle so declared and he believed.
This he had been taught in youth as verity to rest
upon, when of life weary she may — she will await
him at the gate as she did on earth — memory will
recall the forgotten from among the cherubs gone be-
fore to that Arcadia; there, singing the melodies of

Apollo and Diana and the Muses, that never tire;
where Deity presides of whom to know we part with
all below! Severed here reluctantly yet buoyed by
hope of greater gain, more perfect be and satisfied.

This belief in varied phase to Jason would he re-
peat, till Jason saw that reason reeled; was his fellow
sailor sane? Will he, like Deucalion, be perserved
from this wreck, this deluge, or will he as Evadne
throw himself on some funeral pyre, or drown like
Hero in the Hellespont. The Fates are unbending;
why should their wrath on him be piled mountains
high; "Pelion upon Ossa?" No vengeful Furies, no
Nemesis, sought life for life for evils wrought by her!
'twas false.

Vain soliloquies, recalling memories of Historia's
mortals, the true and fabulous. There is no receding
from Nature's laws and fiat! In his anguish he ex-
claimed: "Jupiter! great Jupiter! this life that
opened so propitious now a chaos. Pluto then has
conquered, holds his biprong'd fork aloft with regal
sway—Imperator. He has again struck the earth and
cleft a chasm to Hades to engulf the beautiful and
true! She was not born to die and mix with reeky
clay!" Eurydice, if 'twere possible, where'er she was,
would give him cheer did she but know; how could
she? there is no communing of the living with the
dead!

In life, she knew (in thought) he ever carried her
in his bosom, from earliest thought of woman, ere he
saw her in Diana's train. Then Aurora smiled and
lit the mountain tops of his ambition in planning
paths for her to tread where he in joy would lead her.
Then it was he sang with heart and voice, gave thanks
and praise. Then, tho' absent long upon the ocean
(in thought never was she far away). Together had

they not listened to the rising lark sing its rondelay
of song, its mate the while attentive to its faintest
warblings in the upper air outpouring; it might have
flown to Heaven so high he was; he could not stay
away from her he loved, tho' half the world was in his
vision, full of attractions, but came again to earth to
tell it all in fond affiliation. Thus had Orpheus re-
turned to Athens to recount his travels and tell his
love.

Can no deity proclaim she shall return and speak
as, when her voice at even-tide, as Philomela movest
singing to its love, in sinless innocence she sang; as
he, blissful, praised her joyous carolings, and inter-
changed their thoughts — she, whate'er the theme, so
comprehending, so intuitive, so divine! Such were
his delights in her; 'twas excessive adoration — in
memory they became oppressive and proved expres-
sions of a mind astray.

"Eurydice in Hades," he would say — seek her
he must, he will, and lead her forth from darkness
into light. He will watch at her tomb and woo her
shade if it appear, or as Luna gazed upon Endymion,
and when she wakes be there; then rove the Elysian
Fields with her, and Lethe's stream no more he
feared. There is no place in Tartarus for such as she;
such were his plaintive and intercessant cries.

With such as Jason, pity it did invoke. But who
were those who callous were, who heard at times his
passionate bewailings — he whose smiles once lit ad-
miring eyes of others; they pitied not — they but
seemed to angry grow at his cold looks, averted face
and brief replies to their civilities. They were the
worldly-minded, the motley crowd who disbelieve in
love, such as barter their affections at highest price
or sounding title — semi-sincere worldings who wan-

der and seek they know not what — who fly and ig-
nore a dethroned queen they once flattered, feared and
envied, and cringe to fortune's soiled idols. Eurydice,
dear felicitas! they are the harpies of shame, false
show, duplicity and discord. As tho' present, he
would exclaim, "Avaunt Psyche! Electra away! thy
supposed enchantings are perfumed mildew; thy pre-
tensions vain and odious — away ignis Iris! away
Voluta ceta Gorgons! Helena, Driope, nor Venus
self with all their charms, no semblance have com-
pared to thine; their gaudy plumes but attract the
vulgar Vulcans and the begrimed — could they but
gain one only of thy perfections, 'twould shine a
bright adornment beside their borrowed, ill-gotten
tinsel. They are the consorts of their kind; carrion
creatures, night owls and hawks, with evil eyes alert
to ensnare the unwary innocent." Thoughts and ut-
terings rash his disordered mind evolved; with feverish
eye, wringing hands, bewail'd in broken voice, as tho'
replying to some unseen presence, he would say: " I
will be heard, dread Pluto, in power potential, if
thou art of Hades jailer, be pleased to prove thy right
to stay, or take her hand from mine — mine of earth!
Human, my kith and kin! I'll not believe she's dead
— thine doth lack vitality and are repulsive. Despot,
why with thy fatal power the sapling blight, whilst
hoary trunks fruitless rot, are ready at thy beck — my
branch was beauteous with bloom, that bless'd with
its touch; why should it die? He scorns to make re-
ply!"

But Nature then, as now, had bounds, or the
bruised heart would break or brain congeal. Mor-
pheus benumbed his form, the eye closed, the hand re-
laxed, tears dried upon his cheeks, his strength the
long hours collapse, and sleep disturbed, at last be-

came an opiate. Then as the unwieldy globe swung in
its orbit, came vision after vision; trembling saw he
and heard again " The Midnight Dirge, again saw
he the cortège pass, and noted all the followers. He
knew the air they sang; it was impressed upon his
brain, ' The Judgment Day.' He strove to join its
human lamentation, and he thought 'twas just that he
must cry and share the common doom. He saw them
cheery, going on their way as on a pilgrimage (there
was no need of harp or lyre, for their voices chimed
joyful to a measured step); then Nænia's faint, soft
voice he heard again (as the lull of the winds after
storm, when the tired sailor lays him down to sleep);
it seemed to him to say: ' Behold, mortal; a new day
— Immortality! ' "

IMMORTALITY.

Bright day of peace — Eurydice!
Night and storm have passed away.
And love divine now bids thee stay
To sing in Heaven thy Dorian lay.
Cherubs shall there unfold the scroll
And Heroin's approved extol —
To bless thy name and loving soul
In song and joyous madrigal —
To recompense life's brevity,
And give thee all eternity,
Wherein to joy more happily
Together — dear Eurydice!

Thy sudden light, it passed away,
To shine again as " Dawn of Day,"
For love divine would have thee stay
To make his realm a nightless day —
Angels their choicest garlands bring,
Happy throngs of seraph's sing.
To bless thy name, resound thy fame,
In songs that joy and love proclaim —

There shall no moaning psalmody
Complain to chill the harmony,
But wreathed with smiles of purest ray
And thou his praise and crown and bay
And Orpheus — with Eurydice.

It was like a mother's lull-a-by: Concordia's invocation to the Supreme that could not be denied. He calls her name in sleep, and reason'd " Can dread Pluto hear; can tears to Prosperpine avail; can man conquer thee by daring or liberty obtain for her? Did not Bacchus rescue Semele and Jason rescue Media. Pluto! thine is Proserpine, render Eurydice to me! Erato, Muse of Love, canst thou not open Hades' caves, and from its fabled mysteries bid her come forth — I wait! I wait! Zeus lengthen out the vision. He sped along another Colchis road — he would not be delayed, tho' at Minotaur's sepulchral vault they bid him halt. The guards and ghouls were so absorbed at sight of his wan face that tho' in lost estate and callous to human cries they let him pass. Was it possible? Pluto, too, was silent, for his consort, Proserpine, for Orpheus was pleading. The wicked feel the effect of tears and pity their fellows in distress; she thus her wishes did express, they will prevail. Pluto will not thwart them. Now Erato! with thy heartfelt lays, harp and voice endow that they may touch his heart and he relent. Then music's charm echoes through the concave with piteous sounds and pleas, till Pluto upon his burning dias laid his scepter down; revoked Fate's fiat; revoked his own decree as monarch of the realm; resolved to rehabilitate the one that Orpheus loves — with regal pomp and threat, and legal stipulation. She was to depart with this but one stipulation, most strange and special. " He must suppress all vain feeling, passions and affections given him by Jupiter — his hated brother, the great Imperator of Heaven, and if he fail (and Pluto reasoned that he would) he must destroy his harp that had gained him entrance; depart without her and trespass not in Tartarus again.

The gage accepted, " Upon her face or form to look not until she pass the boundary of his domain."

Orpheus knew not his own strength; his former boasted prowess now was weakness unweaned — Promise! He would accept on any terms. He does. * * * Beauteous still was she as when they first were plighted, for thus in imagination he beheld her. * * * She comes, she comes! Her step he knew, coming in haste his love and loneliness to cheer — she comes in a flood of light, even as a new creation cometh — startling and bewildering — he has forgotten. Alas! he has, for in ecstacy, entranced, he hears her voice and turned about to meet, to clasp her in his arms and gaze upon her face. Oh, weak, impatient, affectionate man! her doom is unrevoked; more vivid than the blinding flash of Cyclop's eye, or Vulcan's thunderbolts, the bolts have fallen; Pluto, frowning, wields again his scepter and closed are the grated gates, with clang so violent that their clash did jar the earth, and Orpheus awoke battling at random, in darkness, saying, " She is not here; she is not here! " His nerves were like his harp, unstrung; his frame in sad abandon. Where were his laurels now, his harp and lyre, once potent with their power and harmony (given him of the Gods)? He had, he thought, entered Hades' depths Eurydice to rescue; but by man's love, impatience, Nature, weakness, lost her; and rashly he exclaimed, "There is no resurrection!" Will he not be calm, it is but defer'ed. " He will never play again." It was the minstrel's final — the retreat began — th⌐

battle lost and he among the slain. He groans and weeps at his defeat. Prestige gone, where shall he hide away?

Such depths of sorrow Cadmus' words cannot translate; those alone who deeply love may dip their pen in tears and write upon his tomb, " Here lies the dust of one who loved."

This is a land of clay, of flesh and blood; he must await time's fiat to meet again in some hoped for, promised, new existence.

These events pass speedily. There is the eternal.

To relieve this mental strain, this monomania and grief excessive, Jason, his captain, his loving friend by Neptune's mystic ties, united gave him a brother sailor's hand. Consider it not strange that there is constancy and love of man to man; the other sex is not loved the less; our mutual joys, trust and tears of this is evidence sufficient. Jason took him to sea again, and with him strove remembrance of the past to banish; 'twas in vain. He pined away, even as Echo for love of Narcissus. Æsculapeus, physician of the Argo, prescribed, but said, " There is no cure for love except reciprocation; delays are fatal."

They were at sea; the voyage was long and stormy. Neptune and the winds were wroth. The Argo was a wreck. With many struggles Jason brought her into port again, where Orpheus' story and identity were in part forgotten. Many cycles of the earth had passed, dates lost and anchor gone; but Orpheus knew he was again near Tempe's vale, where sane and sacred memories lingered. He could not stay away; he haunted all the groves as tho' demented, was shy of man and hid himself from woman's gaze, tho' some from childhood he had known — remembered, both good and true and fair — wandered at times he knew

not where; abruptly talked aloud with Nature when
none were near but flitting birds, fauns and creeping
things, as tho' instructing them incoherently. Æscu-
lapeus was not in error; reciprocation, where 'tis pos-
sible, is the only cure for such a malady; delays are
perilous, the mind may become a wreck, and what
more sad can be, body and mind in collapse, at sight
of which he abandons all his nostrums?

The warders of the shrines knew him, and looked
upon him as one risen from the dead — believed him
dazed, for confused and wild were his replies, erratic
and disjoined. They fed him; they were so directed
from within, and to care for the cave in which he hid
himself or slept and dreamt the time away. He noted
not who furnished his abode. He would sit and gaze
at the moon and weep when clouds obscured her face
— an illusion flickered in the retina of his mind that
her dear profile saw he there, and gazed thereon as
tho' awaiting loves beacon, oblivious of surroundings,
till shivering with the morning's mist he crept within
his cave and fell upon his bed of leaves. Near where
he thought they laid her he brought mosses that he
gathered 'neath the cypress trees — the creeping
myrtle and the blue-eyed violet, ferns and water lilies,
and sometimes the thin-leaved willow that grew and
drooped beside the brook. He fancied that she knew
he laid them there; and as he sighed Eurydice! a
soft æolian sound swept along the reeds near him,
that seemed to whisper " Come!" Prepared he was to
follow, but when again he listened it was gone. Yet
no delusion was that word, come, to him. Night was
his day, for then Philomela came with its plaintive
song that sweetly touched his ear; to this he listened,
a soothing panacea; yet at times it seemed to chide
and bid his grief desist, with its " fi, fi, fi: te-rue, te-

rue, pt! pe-te terue!!" The bee lingers not on a
flower of sweets bereft; the withered flower must bleed
and die — sacred embers quenched; ashes are inurn'd;
who can the vital spark relume; who bring back
the honey of her voice? only memory; it will recall
its tone, her smile and love to him, tho' others may
forget her name — at night, on the morrow and at
noon, and be as caresses past, only his; her voice tho'
heard afar he knew from any other, for it spoke with
childhood's innocence. Aforetime, once, as he drew
near her home he heard her speak his name, looking
heavenward, as if absorbed in thought of him. His
near approach was unobserved, but presently he came
to her, elate and full of joy — joy like to that they
ever feel who sing and breathe and live and love and
idolize!

Lone Dove! thy coo was all anxiety, tho' housed
within till his, thy mate's return; then all within the
Ark was joyous. Love is ever over-anxious! O
timid Deer, thou didst tremble at the twang of the
sped arrow; fly ere its speeding wound thee, thou art
very innocent of harm! And thou, sweet Laverok,
thy song is all of love, for a call from thy mate on
earth doth arrest thy singing midway in its glee; for
thou wilt dive with more than Eagle speed to thy be-
loved — rise higher, she does not call, do not fear, she
listens to thy solo. Had they not together listened
in the glen, and exchanged affections heard therein?
So akin it seemed they were. They are common
things in Nature, given for man's and their own de-
light; they endure but for a day, and die. Such are
intensified in man whose memory and love and soul
survives — evil never sung with so trusting and per-
suasive voice. Shall He weep again; he has not
ceased to weep, tho' tears come not. Shall he rush

into battle as Menelaus at loss of Helen? There is no persuading libertine like Paris for him to slay. Shall he, with deadly hemlock, cheat Cerberus to pass him over Styx? Depart she thought — might it not flow on and land him on some molten wilderness of sand, where his wandering feet would sink to depths beyond compute, where none could extricate? He must await the river's tidal hour ere he sail to the Arcadia of his love.

His walks with her had been where Flora had sent adrift her perfumes, that even now fan his fevered brow with fragrant waft. Would he were there with her again; all else of value seemed to cease to be. He strove to apply the discords and the harmonies he had conceived; speech was inadequate, tongues move not where the stamp of grief is indelible. Those affections, those sorrows, were thaws that melting give responsive echoes in chaste bosoms. Such rhapsodies possessed might, should — would open Eden's Gardens, where man again might enter. It was at such a height of purity and ecstacy with them, when the Olive Crown he gained and Eurydice expired — strange bliss or pain, to die with joy. It was too pure for earth, and perfect, and therefore was recalled. She did not live to tell him of her joy at his success; her demise was an all-sufficient proof. What now was left for him to love? Hover nigh, bright "Dawn of Day," for clouds obtrude ominous presaging thoughts repulsive. His Harp and Lute are out of tune, and Orpheus undone. This, alas! is oft the fate of the good — the truly great. Fate is incomprehensible; the good deceived, awarded with disappointment; hereafter there must be adequate fruition, else (if not so) man, of all creatures, in his life and death, must be deplored; it were better he had not lived! Censor rude! hold! progress is Nature's order of her day, and be so, will, to all eternity. In the final all will be well. Scholars of the Academy, I assert, reiterate, futurity's delay will unfold itself propitious. This life is as Cadmus' Letters, the key to our knowledge of the present and its possibilities, reaching towards the mind, knowledge and soul of The Divine that abides and dies not! Depend not on philosophy alone (ever fallible), 'tis but the alpha to the unknown for which we strive.

Do we not feel pride in the good and true? The wise, the explorers, the heroic, and those who have created our temples and adorned our shrines to instruct the living and honor Jupiter. Such as Musical Orpheus and Sappho — Jason, Theseus, Talemon and Solon? They, tho' dead, still live. They are the conceded princes of the world — equal to Apollo, each an Hercules: remember their achievements, courage and results; they challenge comparison from Historia's pages." Thus was the theme portrayed by Plato, in words and thoughts harmonious, embracing many a song and story. With much solemnity he continued, saying: "Those Bards and Sages live again; and in their children here assembled, resume their vitality with possibilities unbounded!" Plato paused, for now was the proud strain of valor seen in every nerve of his fellow students. Erect stood the untamed sons of Hellena, from Rhodes, from Crete and Cyprus, from Colonies and Islands far and near, ready to man a thousand Argos for any enterprise, to dare — to conquer, or to die! What were floating Pirates or Boreas' storms — what the Harbor bars or guards their stone-closed ports; they will prove that valor is invincible.

The unknown seas now speak of them, our ships pass
to an fro to strange lands, unexplored for ages.   O'er-
thrown are their uncouth Deities.   The soothsayer
and his dupe set free.   No sirens' songs, with tawny
skin, tho' fumed with dust of spice or ointment costly
or color'd daub, hath power to charm or fright.   The
Argo's crew were true to home and kindred.   They
bethought of the voices and forms of Phideas' Models,
that then, as now, our eyes behold; that retain the
charms we cherish and protect.   Such was in part the
Theme that Orpheus sang as the Argo passed the
abode of the sirens — and the Pilot and the crew were
safe.   This scroll is the Mermaid's Song before men-
tioned, as told by Epicurus, found among his pre-
serves, and its preface.   As the Argo passed the en-
chanted isles " They hailed us with, Halloo! Ah, there!
Halloo! "

SONG OF THE SIRENS.

We be Queen Phoebe's daughters all;
To merry men we sweetly call
Come!   Come and see our coral cell.
Adorned with pink and pearly shell.
Here you may clasp a siren's waist
And fruits forbidden pleasure taste.

   As by their rocky isles we sailed, they waved their
fins and flap'd their tails, and then they sang :—

See here, you man, to us oh come,
We'll let you taste of luscious rum
Of nectar made.   Come swig and sip
Grog better than a-board o' ship,
We'll trim your beards and show you where
The pearl and ruby grottoes are.
Ah, there!   See here, man, man!   Mermaid
The foaming surf for love was made.

A water nymph they called Bapta invited us to come ashore, and louder sang than ever :—

See here, you man, my dears, my dear!
Pleasure island is right here;
We'll decorate your necks with pearls;
Come, romp with us, the siren girls.
Our gems and sapphires you may share
And full-blown two-lips kiss a pair.
Now come, oh, come. Ah, there, ah there!
The mermaids' bed is here, here, here!

Brine and bilge-water, boys! The pearls that on their bosoms lay had no place to hide away.

Then sang their queen, in weeds of green -
Come, see my nymphs for sport array'd,
Now, Phoebe's daughters I'm afraid
You don't behave like courtesans.
Let them our new acquaintance make,
Splice the main brace and give and take.
Ah, there! seaman, mermaid!
Come, loll upon our mossy bed.

To stop their gab, " Old Nep." grew mad and awoke a storm from the nor'west, and with a scream they vanished as a dream.

Their arms were flesh, their tails were fish,
They were baiting us, to fill their dish.
With teeth as sharp as tiger claws
They were to fill their hungry maws;
We were to have a coral bed
When dead as herring that are red —
One siren rode upon our anchor bar,
But the pilot swab'd her off with tar.

Those blink-eyed beauties made quite sure we'd furl our sails and go ashore, but the " Yargo " sailed right on her course, as tho' our ears were full o' wool.

And, messmates! " Epi " vouches that the yarn is true.
The landlubbers gaped with open mouths. And the
" Old Salts " laughed, Ha-ha, Ha-ha !

This recital caused a laugh; they had been serious
till then. But when the merriment subsided, Plato
excused himself for this innovation and continued:
" Doves, our mates, with their pure arms, will en-
trance find to hearts at home, and the Hawk and Vul-
ture fail; they live on carrion. · Here Ceres smiles
propitious, and Flora in perfection blossoms. Indus-
try adorns the walks and groves. Heroes walk the
Earth foremost in the van, seeking the Divine. The
whole earth giveth its increase, its fruits abound; Na-
ture's intent, to fill the land and seas with plenty —
with corn and wool, and oil and wine, the promised
recompense of labor; those blessings, these gifts are
trophies, rewards to the industrious and deserving;
for these, Great Jupiter be praised. His approval and
the proofs are here. There are many Argo's heavy
laden, anchor'd off the Piræus, from many open'd
ports, both in and outward bound."

Again the assembled hearers shouted their applause.
* * *   In remembrance of Orpheus, Jason and his
crew, be your praises and mementoes, may they not
even now be cognizant of these sincere and generous
avowals.   The fire-breathing Bulls are conquered.
Mars' blood-stained acres plowed with dragons'
teeth, useless weeds uprooted and buried; instead
thereof, golden grain and liquid opiates richly satisfy.
The Dragon and his guards subdued, and Neptune
Triumphant." Then Plato's fellow students broke out
and sang, as once the Argo's sailors sang :—

A HYMN TO NEPTUNE.

Neptune divine! The ocean is thine;
We mark thy tides, we note their time,
We sail their buoyant waves sublime;
And all their breadth and length define.
    Reign, Neptune! reign!

The earth would show a barren face,
The rocks a blistered shaly waste,
With verdure seared, to blinding dust,
And the winds sweep it of its crust.
    Reign, Neptune! reign!

Thy power hath proud Atlantis seen,
Her domes engulphed in waters green,
Her haughty kings and army braves
Lie deep in thy all-conquering waves.
    Reign, Neptune! reign!

Their continent of earth submerged,
Her lofty mountains mined and surged
And toppled by thy rising tides,
O'er which the Argo sails and rides.
    Reign, Neptune! reign!

The main, the main, 's the road to wealth,
For commerce, luxury and health;
Thy drops refresh the parched ground,
Or human life could not be found.
    Neptune divine, reign!

The Argonauts had cleared the seas of foes, till every wave, from pole to pole, was free. The Tropics opened their spicy treasures, and fruits before untasted, from every clime are ours, whereof Historia hath taken note, and unending praise awards.

When on ocean Orpheus sang of Home, the pigmies and the faithless fled to cover; sirens and seamaids lost their vaunted charms, and Amphitrite, out-of shame, lashed the ocean into foam and hid them

in the surf. The Tritons blew their Conks to decoy.
The Porpoise leapt and the Dolphins' phosphorescent
backs shone with weird light, delusive as Ignis-fires
in the mirk, but Orpheus thought of Hellenes daugh-
ters, to memory dear! Conscious that amid Ocean's
storms Great Jupiter was cognizant and benign, and
held aloft awards for duties done, as up among the
topsails furled they clung. The barren Islands rear-
ward moved; the dawn of brighter days had come —
Pluto's realm of darkness could not bear the light of
progress and not succumb. Neptune's far-reaching
waves again are smooth. Jupiter presides and man's
loyalty receives. Athena issuing Laws, and her peo-
ple jubilant in holdiday attire.

Who could have foretold at such a time the death
of Music's Lord, or so sad a Fate as that befell both
Orpheus and Eurydice? In love for Him she died,
and He, for love and loss of her; yet it is but a sem-
blance, a passing incident, a chill, a stopping of the
breath. Love cannot die. It is believed they are
again joyous with undiminished love in Elysium.
Pluto's shaft, that might have struck a Titan to the
earth, found but a delicate, adoring woman.

Homer! In other words, thy story we repeat.
"Death saw a shining mark gathering flowers in the
meadow lands of Enna, and with his trident cleft the
earth beneath the feet of Proserpine, and Ceres, her
mother, was disconsolate and found her not. She
could have escaped, had she not eaten the forbidden
fruit."

Homer must have heard of Eve and paradise; a
story that the descendants of Abram have on record
long before they went to Egypt. An Hebrew story
of the Earth's Creation; for, not dissimilar is it, as told
by him. " Impatient Orpheus sought to recover Eury-

dice, as Ceres did Proserpine; both were disconsolate and found them not." O fatal day when he was crowned! and passing strange it was that Orpheus played a Dirge ere he closed the final of his skill. Nænia, she who delights in funeral Hymns, suggested

HOMER.

it — she knew that death and change are ever pending, and, to him, urged music's sedatest cadence. There (the effect thereof unknown), 'twas at a time inopportune, so subduing came it, that 'twas as a pall thrown by some gloomy spirit over earth's dependent, loyal creatures, chilling as the winding of a serpent ere it stings. The concourse that but now shouted trembled as tho' Pluto had arrived and changed the Olive into Cypress. By intuition, startled (its effect upon himself), he brought it to a close, and silent was. This by some was thought to be his peroration, for his Harp fell from his hand. What of Her? She had, in excess of joy, as Homer's Proserpine entered the suburbs of the Elysian fields of bliss; Her joy at his success was overpowering, her breathing ceased.

Flora came not at the shrill cry of Proserpine, and Orpheus might have called, and called in vain. A shock, an incident had happened, he knew not what. Yet he bethought 'twas near the spot where Eurydice had stood; 'twas well he did not, or in passion's violence he would have brought her forth from peril, tho' Cerberus barred the path, or perish'd then and there.

He who had made the Islands and the woods to move — the rocks to roll. The carnivorous to forget their hunger, the vile to listen, to regret their lost estate and lack of purity — could he not succeed again? Will he not dare to make the attempt to enter any where, and rescue her? His Harp and voice again were in accord, drawn at times so fine, to such a plaintive pitch, that the hitherto indifferent Ghouls— even the Furies, laid aside their nature's and serious became. What will not Harmony and Love o'er-come?

Eurydice — the pure of heart! She perceived from whom came all the joys of earth to her; in him they all were concentrated. Wherein did he sin? To worship her; none were so without defect; possessing all the perfections that Athena, Diana, Juno or Venus boasted.

Helena, the Spartan, was a wife; She, a love-con-

fessed, an affianced one. Oh, he will, if the Fates
deter not, besiege the crater of Hades and rescue her;
who shall delay; who hinder?

Again in vision he was rapt, but journeyed on till
strange lugubrious mutterings of the doomed were
heard, and again were silent, for his Harp was plead-
ing in piteous petition, with words more piteous; they
were bent persuasive to powers within, to open callous
ears till they become susceptible; that he, the sup-
pliant, bending low, might arise and entrance gain.
Obtain such pity as in the Hebrew story Adam gave
to Eve; who, driven from gardens of ease to a wil-
derness of toil, content departed to bear and abide
the doom, if not deprived of her.

She had passed over Lethe's stream, and he will
dare to follow. * * * Then, then he thought, he
sang and play'd continuous, seraphic, till the doomed
in Tartarus rattled and clank'd their shackles in ap-
plause and Pluto laid down his dichtomous fork in
fret — surfeited with melodies and flatteries of love —
pleas and petitions that tyrants dread and despise un-
der pressure, gruffly suspend law and power.

Music's persuasive key had won the obdurate to
unbar the ponderous gates—Minotaur's dread cavern
open to the abyss — sulphurous fumes arise from Vul-
can's forge; they do not injure; they flame a lurid blue
above his path in their escape towards Proserpine's
strange temple, where by right divine Pluto holds his
court.

Indifferent He, to entrance or exit of mortal, be he
man or slave; can he not make or unmake; command
and be obeyed in his own imperial domain!

Tyrants at times test the sincerity of subordinates
and their allegiance prove. He hears Pluto debate:
" Is Love Jupiter's primal trait, bestowed on mortals

and held by man as a hallow'd verity! He hath en-
tered here for love; what will he not do in his per-
sistency; he will besiege the prison house of Pluto!
Pluto will be dethroned by Love." Yet she, for
whom Orpheus pleaded — ventured, was pure as Di-
ana; fit companion for a God, a work divine, in its
self complete. Pluto condescendingly bade him look
into futurity; the untravel'd destiny was thrust before
him, delusive. 'Twas brilliant, but momentary. There
within the great hall at Altis saw he His own statue,
a central figure surrounded by Historias, Victors of
the Olympic Games. The renowned of fame. He
standing on a pedestal as high as Apollo's. It was the
Nation's Mausoleum of the departed, that the Sages,
the Graces and the Muses decorate with apt and ap-
propriate devices. The Fame-honored were in mo-
tion, as tho' about to speak — as He awoke, at sound
of his own voice in discussion with them, saying,
" What are chisel'd stone but soulless vanities of the
living? They give sepulchers, erect colossal statues of
the Dead, and turn aside, refuse to see the wants and
penury of the living. Was He worthy, must he
bridge the chasm alone, deny a fault he would not,
nor commit. Alas, who is faultless, who is sinless?
If sin she had, let it be attributed to him, he so de-
sired.

She had ascended beyond where the Lark soareth,
where guileless cherubs pose in innocent abandon.
When on earth He sang the birds corrected their mis-
takes and mutely listened; 'twas to her joy unalloyed
to hear, faultless as Erato's poesy. Deíope and all the
beautiful deign'd to smile upon " The Young Apollo."

The Muses, Judges in all the schools of Art, ap-
proved the meritorious award, as tho' faulty were all
competitors but him, and he, perfect was alone.

Who can define the dreams of mortals, or the outcome of life predict? One act, nay, a word in error taken, may dethrone a king and prostrate his strong citadel! They say Eurydice, at the Arena, shed tears of gratitude to those who gave the applause, to requite, as best she could, their choice and condescension. They perceived, she Loved. Whilst He the while, in his theme absorbed, sang on, yet 'twas to her he sang, for no other heart or ear was it intended; it was, in part, His Love Confession, for so the final stanza ran.

WHEN LOVE IS DEAD.

Tune: " Bonny Doone."

Tell, tell me not, that earth is fair,
Where golden grain is waving,
That limpid waters onward flow,
The flowers and grasses laving.
Oh! what are they, or sacred shrine,
Or fountains clear, or laurel grove?
They all are blurred and colorless,
When silent is the voice of love!

The intent listeners imagined this to be a Dirge, and so it proved to be, for at its sadly sweet and holy close Eurydice fell into a matron's arms, where they fanned her pallid face, but fanned in vain. The spirit had departed and to the rear her form was borne. They thought she would recover — conflicting were the immediate cause assigned.

When she was at his side and whispered " Sing again "— then as he sang it seemed to her the zephyrs breathing ceased — the leaves were still, creatures mute and motionless, the stars all aglint. Afar away the rippling streams beckon'd the Neriades, and they, from brooks and rivers peered, and would have left

their watery abodes, had Neptune been away, to
nearer come and listen.   Dear and perfect confidence
— peace of mind, such only as the forgiven feel, that
have offended.   Then it was he believed himself in
Eden's gardens, where they did wander.

But now he was but a wreck'd vessel, driven by
conflicting winds and waves — and again he dreamt
that mind-absorbing theme — the rescue.   Again
he saw the gates of Hades open (dread place).   He
stood within and trembled, waiting till announced.
The Tribes in Tartary fell back to give him place; a
stranger guest to them was He, their toothless jaws
agape, wondering — strange miscellany, for Cupid was
there; and Venus, she has right, she is everywhere
Goddess.   She boldly laughs at Pluto, as Cupid, her
offspring is standing by, with his bowstring loose,
its arrow, having pierced the callous heart of Pluto —
even He.   Love had conquered.   Now Love was ex-
emplified.   He forthwith revoked the doom of Fate,
as, with stentorian voice, " Orpheus," he proclaimed,
" she shall arise ! "   And renewed Auroral lights from
Vulcan's fires threw rosy tints to light the way.   O,
joyous !   They are coming to his wedding.   Diana's
horn awoke the welkin — the Hounds are out —
Eurydice was foremost in the Train of Nymphs.   He
heard the echoes ; nearer they approach.   She is com-
ing !   Coming to him, as 'twere, to escape to heaven?
No ! 'twas to meet and Liberty regain?   So real, so
startling were its commingled sounds, that in excite-
ment's ecstacy, He turned to see how near she was,
and be the first to greet her ; and again, thereby, his
memory and self-possession lost — as tho' blind and
deaf, with promises forgotten.   Oh, rash, foolish, fatal
look, He turned to guard and clasp her form, but the
Furies in derision stormed with hiss and scream, as

they hurried him along as one in banishment con-
demned. Pluto's stipulation broken, and the outer
gate is open for his exit, that gaunt Charon, held ajar
until he passed, and Cerberus, in his kennel, thrice
howled in the gloom. He awoke, as one fleeing from
peril, a dazed wanderer, bewildered in a thorny maze.
And vaguely he exclaimed, " It was a Dream."

Dreams are delusions; the troubled body's sense of
pain, a confused medley of chaos that usurps the
mind, and the realities of life are all deranged thereby.
He would that he could dream no more; 'twill lead
him to disregard and doubt the real. Alone, with
stringless Harp, his Lyre broken, his crown a bauble
— his Fame unnoted. How could he have thought
for happiness it was essential! His curls, through
which the sun shone as they hung upon her bosom,
now, by the winds and briars matted. The hosts that
at the Games gave plaudit and applause gone, fled
with Cupid to tropic skies, where wantons bud and
blossom, and dissipate the time away; he could not
call them friends; how cold they had grown, they used
to bask at his table — laud his skill — praise his
songs, even to repetition. O, then, his common
speech was Iambic — Dactyl or spondee in faultless
measure, and, like to Jason, with ever open purse.
Compare not Him to them, with their glib tongues —
court flatterers, insincere — pfau-birds, that obstrusive
press their insipid inquiries and laugh and joke, in-
sinuate and mock his woeful look.

Then did he feel the world had ceased to Love and
Deucalion's Flood should come again; at best their
words were chill and formal; such as the Temanite
gave Job of old, with argumentative philosophy, va-
ried, meaningless and vapid — Orpheus dared not
Great Jupiter malign! Companionless (he desired

none), He for solace and silence, sought the inanimate — the woods and groves, where the Hemlock is always green; fit place to screen the wounded from pursuit; there would he discover their secret balm or poison, and (if peace come) in the meadows find hidden flowers and note their perfumes, forms petals and pollens and their varied shell and shield that protects the germ, life to perpetuate and wonder, and adore their Creator.

There he would meet the timid Fauns, and let them stare at him. Wander aimless and alone. Nature's inmates will not molest — some cave will give him shelter; he will feed with them on leaves. Shy creatures will visit him — they never fled when he drew nigh! A coney with its young once lay upon his feet; with much ado it was he did not injure them. The birds would sing close to their mossy nests, as if to show him their hymeneal abode. They awoke for the moment responsive fellowship. He was conscious of their pity; he could commune with them. To them he sang his plaint :—

Tune: " Bonny Doone."

Sing to thy mate, sweet bird again;
Repeat it through the leafy glen.
If she believe thy love refrain,
She will, she will! be happy then.
There was a time, that now is gone
When in my song I sang of love,
Mine heard a call imperative
To come and join the choir above.

Now, as yon lark beyond the clouds,
Who calls to earth so fondly,
I would be rising heavenward
To her who loved me dearly —

To living ears those notes resound,
With fondest trills of feeling;
They gurgle, whistle, warble now,
And all love's chimes are pealing.

Brouse, timid deer, on mountain top;
My arrow shall not pierce thee.
Diana's hounds are leash'd in sleep,
Or they might tear thee fiercely —
But haste thee on! why linger here
From her who loves thee dearly?
May-hap, alike, she's dead and gone,
As mine — and left thee lonely.

No! tell me not that earth is fair,
Where golden grain is waving,
That limpid waters onward flow,
The flowers and grasses laving.
Oh! what are they, or sacred shrine,
Or fountains clear, or laurel grove?
They all are blurred and colorless,
When silent is the voice of love.
    Eurydice! Eurydice!!

Morpheus, with his recipe for sorrow, soothed and kindly bathed his brow with drops from Lethe's stream. The perfumed zephyrs fanned the hectic flush — Nature, tired, more firmly closed his eyes, and turbulent thought was calm again. Tears adown his cheeks had coursed; tears relieve, then may follow tranquility — pain's estoppel — symbol of obliteration of sin and pain and thought. Blessed Jupiter! Be it so! It doth not shut out memory and joy and Love, hope and they awake again. No more of Hades — all is placid now; so long he slept that Urania and Somnus in thought's vision brought him scenes of others' sorrows to relieve, to mitigate his own — some of which he had heard the poets in story tell and glorify. They troop before him. " Endymion

and Luna upon Mount Latmus." Luna's face was pale
with watching, and Juno's with anger flushed — poor
shepherd, thou didst aspire too high, thou were re-
buked.   Pride, wealth and beauty were above thy
sphere.   Then came Leander, self-reliant, who nightly
came and swam to Hero (he sighed in sleep piteously),
the jealous Nereides have let him drown.   She came
to meet him at the sandy shore, where she could
wade to him.   She knew him true, that he would
venture — rude Boreas with clouds frowned.   A
storm was on the Pont and baffled all his skill.   O
Love! what wilt thou not do?   What not attempt.
She waited long; depart she would not — her bewail-
ing never ceased till she embraced his form upon the
beach, and, with him clinging, was by the receding
waves submerged.   Joy at last! parted they were not.

   Then thought he of Polyzena (filial daughter to re-
deem the body of a brother from the chariot wheels
of an unfeeling victor, even to wed him), she, Priam's
daughter.   He was to restore the bruised and lifeless
Hector (she had consented).   Oh, she would thereby
alleive the sorrow of her honored Parents, and Andro-
mache's anguish and other kindred that Loved dear
Hector for his valor, worth and manhood.   With
streaming eyes downcast, led by her mother, Hecuba
— she beside him, took the place assigned.   Oh!
what a marriage, a Lion with a Lamb — but the Gods
forbade.   Paris! thy faults thou didst in part an-
nul, when thou didst slay the lewd barbarian.   Op-
portune moment — successful aim, to drive thy
pointed arrow through his hoof, his vulnerable part,
and pin him to the earth — what tho' they burn Her
body on His pyre to appease his manes.   His Spartan
Chiefs vaunted that if sacrificed to him, Achilles would,
in the Elysian fields of bliss, enjoy her forever.   That

existence is not for such as he! The Fates have seized upon his heel, hold and dip him perpetual in Styx baptismal stream. His name, tho' falsely boasted brave, is now despised, and Hector and Polyzena honored and adored, and at the verdict Orpheus smiled in sleep. Then came Sappho, once so praised, so wise, so beautiful. Mistress of the Muse, who had so lately Love's songs sung, that did elicit praises from Poets and from Princes — from broken rest she came distraught with Love. Love of Phaon. Love, tho' made evident in delicate avowal — unrequited. She, weird-like, strayed upon the Lucadian Rock (in fate's defiance), upon the brink of which she sat to scold the Moon — tear her hair, deranged and raving, fell into the Ocean's depths. In restless agitation he sprang to save her, and awoke, with every limb in tremor.

Then came an hour, ah then! his thoughts reverted to his mother — next in dear remembrance — ever Dear! who in past early lull-a-bys first kindled harmony and music's flame within him; long before his teachings by Apollo. She, who purity inculcated and the foundation laid of manhood, for she upon him left her noblest impress, they still were his, tho' dead she was. Break thy Harp Philomon; Hermes, unstring the Lyre. Music is mute when Love is dead!

Deem it not unmanly, He sighed, for a return of her maternal care, her guileless Love, on whom to lean and hear — listen to her sage and womanly condolence. Who shall guide him now — no Mentor — Pilotless, anchor lost, reason wreck'd — upon a shoreless, stormy sea.

Weep for the disappointed — for Sappho, the Sweet Singer, for Hero and Leander, and for Orpheus and Eurydice!

　　And Greece and Athens have other games they cele-
brate resumed again near Tempe's valley, where He
had eclipsed the assembled Champions and bore away
the prize — a most notable event!

ATTICA'S FEAST OF BACCHUS

Had been announced 'mid preparation vast to out-
do the past in show and sport, and grand licentious-
ness.　But proved to be a hollow mockery, a senseless
medley, a rabies' revel — Degenerate Greece!　Bar-
barians from far and near had landed, and pollute
the classic land, fill the Arena, desecrate the groves;
invade the sacred temples and make a pandemonium.
Wonder not that the Oracles therein ceased to foretell
events.　They feed and leave foul stains and scraps
at the base of every statue, and camel-like carry their
hampers, greasy with travel, that reek and breed con-
tagion.　They were assigned a place, where the wind
would carry their fume seaward.

BACCHANALIAN PROCESSION.

　　The procession! the procession!　It comes heralded
by Trumpet and Drum and Shout.　Bubona with her
white oxen garlanded in leading strings led by beau-
teous children, with reins of flowers and ribbons, in
mimicry of a sacrifice, to placate and prove Great Ju-
piter had been propitious, followed by the shepherds

with their long-fleeced sheep and goats, and other caged and uncaged creatures. Next Autumnus, with her fruits of earth. Harvesters, with their sheaves of grain high piled on wains. Peasants of the fields, with their barley bread and figs, apples of Carthage, oranges, lemons, sprigs of clustering filberts, branches of almond, with their pink blossoms, with mulberry and grape. Patient industry, a worthy sight displayed to swell a Bacchanalian pageant.

BACCHANALIAN PROCESSION.

These were followed by the Mimic Muses, and each her calling symbolized. They were led by Mars, the callous, whose step did crush the atoms in his path. With axe and spear, fire and sword, as tho' coming from a recent slaughter, strutting as tho' glorying in deeds of blood. Appropriate, followed Tragic Melpomene with her dagger drawn, and Tacita the silent, with finger press'd upon her lips, and Muta, with fear and utterance dumb. She pointed to a passed path stained with blood and ashes. Tears lay upon her cheeks, ready to fall. Next, by her dress and lank visage, came a widow, dragging a tired child, shoeless and refractory — she would! despite of Herald, have her say. She with pale, thin lips, said in bitterness of scorn (her lament and dissent of unrighteous war) :—

THE WAR-WIDOW'S LAMENT.

Behold the Spartans' Heliot warriors!
This is Mars and these his followers.
Himself and shield were thrown from heaven,
And for his symbol fire was given,
With wolves and vultures 'graved thereon,
Barbaric things to look upon,
Bringing blood stains upon the nation,
Death, cruelty and desolation!
Let those who wage the quarrel fight,
Doth not weird famine thee affright?
Jove filled the heavy ears with corn,
That smiled propitious, all are gone!
The fruitful fields seemed overjoyed,
This, Mars and horse and fire destroyed —
For food the helpless faint and moan,
The wounded bleed, the cripples groan.
And now they brag that Mars is brave.
Who dares dispute, is not a slave!
Here are the proofs that war is wild,
Unjust to man, to wife and child.
With disrupt homes, with thread-bare dress,
That scarce doth hide their nakedness.
Come child! and see thy father's grave,
The state admits that he was brave.
Compelled to leave our home and thee,
Whom he had known so recently.
Our wedded consecrated love
Was all in thee — I'll faithful prove!
Poor wounded warrior — all alone,
The wolves have heard thy dying groan.
And thus he died? 'twas hard to part;
He left me with a broken heart.
O braver far is he who toils
At home, and shares not pirate spoils.
Minerva, guide us! let right be shown,
Then courage will defend its own.

She sorrowed much; 'twas Love's recall
And memory's grief the tears let fall.
Her hand the child pressed to its face,
Looked up more firm to cope with fate.
Bellona's mercenary troops march'd on,
And mock'd the words of her harangue.

Then came Milo and Ægean, the boxers and the
wrestlers. Men of sturdy build and sinewy arms and
stony fists, to throw the javelin, quoit or heavy bar —
followed by the sound of lung and lithe of limb to
outspeed Mercury, to running gear denuded. The
boxers bruised and bled like slaughtered carcases.
The wrestlers trick'd and kicked, fell maimed and
lamed, and the vulgar called it sport. But of which
Plato expressed his opinion, more in contempt than
in anger, as he said:

THE BOXERS AND THE WRESTLERS.

They live their little day and pass away,
Conquered at last by others, vile as they —
What vanity of vanities!
Brutal, without humanities.
To wrestle, kick and plunge and mall.
And cripples make of those who fall.
Tho' e'er so beauteous, make a wreck.
And throw him tho' it break a neck —
Or mar his face with stony fist,
His mother oft so fondly kissed —
Hear foul-mouth slang in banter boast,
Of their piasters won and lost —
Bragging drones that loll in the sun,
And the working bees impose upon;
They are the buzzards of the plain,
Carrion seekers shaming man's name.
Keep well aloof from such as they,
With such base tricksters do not play.
Do not degrade thy country or clan,
Fellow strident thy hand — be a man!

6

Let the bulls rush, the canines fight
And animals of lower type.
Thy self-respect and name maintain,
Reserve thy strength for righteous fame.
Then shall the record be of thee —
" He did his duty "— manfully!

Then followed the Tritons with their trumpeters,
that blew their distended cheeks with blear-eyed
straining; and goat-like satyrs leapt and wrestled
with their horns and cloven feet; and buffoons and
loons and clown straddled along with grimace and
painted face, and harlequins burlesque performed their
parts to gaping, grinning crowds, and merry Momus
held his sides till with laughter overcome — the rural
boobies guffaw'd their fill.

Then came Orythia, Amazon's queen, and Alacto
with her company of man-women; Hippona bold,
straddling the quadruped, and other Furies in dis-
guise of modesty devoid; then followed a troop of
barely-clad adventurers to show their graceful form,
their knack at pose and posture. When Venus passed,
as she arose from the sea, supported by the Nereides,
it was commented and appeared absurd that the bald-
pate men, even the Judges, to see the sight, strove
more excitedly than did the young. They offered as
excuse, " That they with sight defective have to take
a nearer look."

An interval, but then came bevies of fair girls and
youth garlanded and gay, and the God Bacchus in
Nature's best array. A naked boy, naked as Cupid,
dimpled, plump and rosy, sat with vine and ivy trail-
ing, holding his scepter like a king; his golden car by
subdued lions drawn, Silene, his mother leading them.
She was there to hold them in check lest they should
rampant grow and destroy both Bacchus and his wor-
shipers; and they, with band and voice sang merrily :—

BIRTH OF VENUS.

DECORATING THE GARDEN STATUE OF BACCHUS.

BACCHUS IS KING.

Tune: "Swiss Boy."

Here we come with thy grapes, ruddy boy,
  From the vale of Ny-a-sas' fair land.
Where the sun paints the clusters with joy:
  See they purple our lips and our hands —
We will scatter the seed at thy feet,
  And train all their tendrils to grow.
For each globe holds a delicate sweet,
  That our presses with nectar o'erflow.

Then merrily sing, for Bacchus is king,
He gives us the vine and its fruits that we bring.
    Evan! Evoe! Evan! Evoe!!

Shout your joy, shout for joy! come and share,
  He hath open'd his odorous store,
And his vine blossoms fill all the air,
  'Till enamored our senses adore —
We'll drink from the sweets of his cup,
  We'll invite all the jovial to share;
Then our tongues as the liquid we quaff,
  Will pay court to the young and the fair.

Then merrily sing, for Bacchus is king,
He gives us the vine and its fruits that we bring.
　　Evan! Evoe! Evan! Evoe!!

We will laugh, joyous laugh, ha, ha, haa!
　For its life-giving essence imparts
A bliss that no sorrow can mar,
　As it lightens and brightens all hearts —
We'll partake of this life-giving wine,
　As our festival time passes by,
And when life's sun is on the decline,
　We'll sip its sweet perfume and die.

Then merrily sing, for Bacchus is king,
He gives us the vine and its fruits that we bring.
　　Evan! Evoe! Evan! Evoe!!

BACCHANALIAN PROCESSION.

And so they passed along; but then came, Oh, shame! who can depict the opposite?

Discordia's Harpies of contention, clanging their Bacchanalian tabors, led by Acratus reeling, that the vine branches that they jointly carried, grape sprinkling the way, kept from falling. They marched with ribald shout and song.

The Bacchanalian Chorus.

Avo Avoa! To Bacchus and the vine. The drums and timbrels beat, the brasses clang'd and Pan piped derision's music in buffo. The choristers sang and croaked the Bacchanalian chorus :—

DRUNK-FULL.

Avaunt, spectre, morose!
Fill up the bowl
A fig! for the toll!
Fill up! jolly Jocose?
The vintage is on,
This is our song,
May Bacchus the revel prolong,
    Avo! Avoa!
May Bacchus the revel prolong!

And the swollen goats pranced in unison.
Then sang Acratus, decorated, amid his grape and vine leaves full, but with utterance faulty :—

TO BACCHUS AND THE VINE

Here's to wine! the ru-ruby wine,
  That has ran down my throat.
Wine has no dregs if it is fine,
  And neither had-it-ought!
    Hic! Hic! Avo! Avoa!
  To Bacchus and the vine.

When it is new, it-it is too thin,
  As posset, d-d'solved to pap,
Fill me a flagon to the brim,
  Before I take my nap.
    Hic! Hic! Avo! Avoa!
  To Bacchus and the vine.

When it is old and I've a cold,
  A cold I always dread.
I fill my bowl with so'thing old,
  To, to, tinge my nose — a red
      Hic! Hic! Avo! Avoa!
      To Bacchus and the vine.

Wine! hic! will cure 'most anything,
  Except to cure my thirst.
It gives disgusto while I sing,
  That empty is my purse.
      Hic! Hic! Avo! Avoa!
      To Bacchus and the vine.

Wine never was a headache cure,
  But good for squirms or shakes,
It's awful good to cause a snore,
  See adders crawl — and snakes.
      Hic! Hic! Avo! Avoa!
      To Bacchus and the vine.

Now it is late, I scarce can prate,
  Or follow my own nose —
I find wine, will intoxicate
  May-hap, turn up my toes.
      Hic! Hic! Avo! Avoa!
      To Bacchus and the vine.

'Necrean now tho' thou sing or prate,
  'Nd I'll just hold the bottle.
Wine surely will, evaporate,
  If out is left the stopple.
      Hic! Hic! Avo! Avoa!
      To Bacchus and the vine.

Dizzy became Anacreon and gag'd and strove to
vomit forth a swallow'd seed from his mellow throat,
but stumbling fell and broke the empty bowl. Tiletus,
his fellow-mate, drunk, smear'd with lees, corpulent
and red, sat riding his Pegasus (an ass with wings),
it should have been a horse; it was neither; it was a

mixture (wings); it was his feet that flew at the striplings that tickled him behind; but on Tiletus clung to mane and tail, wearied out the kicker and wasn't thrown, tho' bareback'd was the mule.

Then to their separate tents they did depart, wearied with their own folly, whilst others sought the less frequented groves to feast it out among the revelers.

" With the dancers and the dicers, and the * * *" Plato check'd himself and said, " The horses and the chariot races closed without a broken bone or dislocation." Then, with more serious face continued, as tho' returning to the Theme of Tragedy:

" Oh, ill-hap, that where the Bacchi pitched their tents Orpheus should be found! Orpheus thought himself a lone, wreck'd sailor — sail and chart and comrade's gone, lash'd to a broken helm in a boundless sea — drenched — saw the vivid bolts of Vulcan pierce the gloom, as tho' Neptune and Pluto wrangled for precedence with angry Boreas roaring; himself in chaos, doom pending.

" The exhausted body a strange effect produced, the cloudy mind was clearing — the climax came, for a ray of reason had come to him — ' Great Jupiter was kind! '

" From that doubt, that agony of regained reason, he sank upon a stone exhausted, with hands buried beneath his face to further reassure himself of his existence; and then, arising, like a wounded Greek, to battle still.

" He felt the walls of his abode exclaiming, ' These are rocks; is it not so? I was in a storm; a ship-destroying storm; I'm not at sea! this is not the Argo! Yet this I know, that whene'er this mortal dies the part Immortal will be received among the Gods! '

" He heard the discordant shouts without — of the

Bacchanalian revelers — and thought of the doomed
in Tartarus.   He would prepare (he was preparing)
for a celestial voyage; happy faces flit along the way;
he would leave this cave and take the voyage; he had
fought his last battle unwounded; peace to him had
come — he was sane — no face was half so tranquil —
homeward bound, his log written, ready to report.
He had within himself premonitions of approval; he
heard a familiar voice call him; he had heard that
voice before in dreams bid him to follow — so certain
was he that she spoke that he aloud replied, ' Eury-
dice, I come! I come! '

   " He is conscious of his surroundings; he is chill,
for he drew the fragments of his garments close
around him, and questioning, sadly sang :—

                          Tune: " Robin Adair."

        Why in this cave am I,
        My friend not here;
        Good Jason did not die,
        Let him appear!
        Where is the jovial crew,
        So prompt his will to do,
        I would that I but knew
        They were so dear!
        Where is Eurydice,
        My own betrothed?
        Where, say? if dead she be,
        Is her abode?
        Why was I rent with pain,
        I remember it again?
        Her absence turned my brain,
        I had lost the road.

   " Music of Terpsichore, with laugh and scream and
voice of woman in delirium, their Bacchanalian shout
comes very near.   He had not been disturbed within

his cave until they entered, and found him there. It was a discovery where search would seem in vain. For a moment there was mutual astonishment; they stared at him and drew back, and then boldly in numbers entered and dragged him forth, exclaiming ' 'Tis Orpheus!' weak and unsightly as he was they clung upon him, maudlin; they bade him play upon his harp again as was once his wont and forte. 'Play, play!' they screamed, 'and we will dance and raise Baalphegor,' but he heeded not, and when persuasion failed and threat had no effect —

"He thus addressed them: 'Seest thou not that I am not, of thy company. Intrude not upon a recluse, a man of sorrow! But would'st thou have man believe thy virtues, his above — he notes thy constant journeys to the shrines, even to Diana's! Listen, oh listen! To teach his children thou wert given, to gently guide them to Elysium or earthly happiness, whilst he at plough or mart or sea, toils to obey the divine decree cheerily!'

He feels repaid when he discerns,
Maternal care when he returns;
  Would'st thou to virtue lead thy child
  Be not with drunkenness defiled —
Let evil wine ne'er stain thy lip,
For virtue's feet it oft doth trip.
  Then — lost to modesty and shame,
  What charm can wipe away the stain.
Each lewd masked tempter will arise,
And thy loose wallowing despise —
  In ribald sport, mock and disclose,
  Thy shame — thy weakness all expose
Believe — no rose-lip'd Bacchant maid,
Can guard her charms if thus arrayed.
  No reeling fumed inebriate she,
  Can claim Diana's purity.
The sweet emetic is a tempting snare,
That leads to shame — to death — beware!

"They had gather'd as hounds around a wounded
deer, with eyes aflame at close of hunt, at scent of
blood, for he had scarce closed his good advice —
faith and belief in woman (advice well meant), ere
they sprang upon him — spat in his face, were furious;
tore his hair, stript him with their claws and threw
him to the earth — tugged at either arm with drunkard
strength; and he, of whom 'twas said fear'd not man,
was in their delirious clutch, powerless as a wounded
warrior in the midst of hungry wolves, and like the
wolves they bayed at him, saying :—

"'Who was Philomela? Pure as Diana! ravished
by Tereus;' another cried 'Who was Helena! (beauti-
ful as Venus) abducted by Paris;' another cried out
'Who was fair Dido (a deceived Diana) by Æneas
deserted;' 'Who tuneful Sappho (delight of Diana
in song) deceived by faithless Phaon;' and with
shriek, they cried 'Who tore Eurydice from Diana's
shrine? — 'twas Orpheus!' And Orpheus heard their
several indictments against man and was silent, but
when he was himself arraigned his tears well'd up,
and faintly he replied, 'Woman! in this thou art false!
false as thou art cruel!' Then Circe struck him with
her sickle and he bled — resistance none was offered,
except in words—'Shame Dione thou art false as
Fabula — Bacchi revelers do not thyselves unsex.
Would'st thou find mercy, be * * * while he was
yet speaking Debauche press't her hands upon his
mouth until he ceased to breathe — as wasps upon a
bare-neck'd boy they with obeluses pierced him.
"Mercy! in a shoal of sharks a drowning sailor
finds none; they hack him, they tear his limbs, and
another Adonis dies. They had suck'd the blood of
the grape as vampires till demoniac they became.

DEATH OF ORPHEUS.
(By permission of Gebbie & Co., Philadelphia, Pa.)

" But such as they had often looked with sensual
eyes upon him; displayed in vain their charms in
varied temptings — semi-modest.   They called him
in derision 'Narcissus, in love with his own shadow.'
Midas' daughters had glittered their finery, taunted
him with words unseemly.   They, knew not love!
They derided the name of Love and flung their taunts
and mockings at him.   Strip'd the leaves from his
faded trophies and flung them in the Lotus pond.
Some, but oh, how few, were there who felt one pity-
ing pang as they saw his torn and lifeless form.

" The Dryades of the woods fled in terror, for Mel-
pomene had closed the Tragedy.

" Jason had been apprised but came too late.   He
tenderly raised him from the earth and bore away
his body.

" Shade of harmonious Orpheus!   As the dial by
clouds obscured no more doth tell where it was shone
upon, we miss thy light, but time nor sun has not
effaced the memory of thy love and gentle life.

" Where are the Bacchi and their orgies?   Re-
morse's memories flash'd athwart their path with their
annoy, and they have perished in their lair.   They rot
in the earth as drones and gluttons inglorious, and are
forgotten, and are, as tho' they had not been.

" The morrow came; then the Oracles unloosed
their tongues.   The Muses have come forth to herald
for all time the loves of Orpheus and Eurydice.   Their
joint and glorious fame in their Unsullied Love.

" They made his tomb — design'd his statue for
Minerva's Temple — its colossal figure stands con-
spicuous.

" Jason, his constant, latest friend, rendered his
eulogy in recognition of his worth, his perfections, his
manhood and his faith in Divine love;" that Plato in

brief repeated as " Our ideal man — one like unto
Orpheus there is none."

"Euterpe and her choir of friends were there; she
sang a dirge in which they joined at close of each re-
frain. 'Twas of joyous import, tho' in solemn meter
rendered :—

A DIRGE TO ORPHEUS AND EURYDICE.

No! they are not dead,
What e'er our lips have said.
Let not your hearts be sad,
They have risen! from the dead!
Rejoice, rejoice! They have risen from the dead!

Orpheus and Eurydice!
Our memories doth again
Revivify thy name,
For as lovers we rejoice
At the never-ending fame.
Rejoice, rejoice! At thy never-ending fame!

Now endless be thy love,
For love can never die.
This we on earth believe,
Thy souls can never grieve —
But sing and praise eternally,
Great Jupiter above.
Rejoice, rejoice! They never more can grieve!

Inheritance Divine!
Greater gain than olive crown,
To gain Elysium!
Love divine, thy faith will meet,
And thy betrothal be complete;
Where parting is unknown.
Rejoice, rejoice! They have gained Elysium.

" Erato and other gentle poets say: ' Philomela
sings nightly at his tomb in remembrance of his sweet

TOMB OF ORPHEUS.

songs : ' Birds of unpretentious plume, sing on ; thy notes, tho' wordless, are fond comfort to innocent ears — to those who love — sing to them.   They are now omniscient where such symphonies are heard in continuous change, that never cloy as they flow and echo through fields Elysian, where bliss is most complete.

PLATO.

He is thine, Eurydice ; to thyself take him ! All lovers say amen !

"They have found that realm, doubtless, where the human and divine are happily conjoined.   The schools cannot solve its near or distant sphere — 'tis too profound for man yet not beyond belief — Great Jupiter! confirm our faith in its reality, make glad the earth, let it be fruitful; ripple waters to the ocean, bear our ships of commerce. Come bud and blossom, herb and flower and add thy joy! fields with thy grain the harvest bring, and man give thanks and praise. Creatures thy natures satisfy; sing, feed, bound and live, thine is an evanescent day, brief and to pass away. But for man the continuous harmonies of Divine Love live on — live on! for whom?

" It was announced, and reason doth approve, ' The wicked shall be, in futurity, as tho' they had not been; but the pure in heart shall never die.' Dost thou comprehend?" And many hands in affirmative were raised.

Thus continued he to philosophize on Immortality to the close of his lecture. This ' reading from Homer,' saying in peroration: "I would not have that belief from my mind removed for all the world!"

Then arose Socrates (the wise) commenting on the poem (in epilogue) and the thoughts involved said: ' Except Great Jupiter himself, your gods and goddesses are inferior things, have no soul, are not divine — unworthy they of worship are. Less than mortal have mere semblance; shadows of deformities that with the light vanish as fiction and darkness before the font of Truth and Light, think no more of them, they recede to Erebus.

'If it were possible that a perfect man should come to the earth and vile would destroy him.'

He then, with upraised face, in supplication said:

'Father Jupiter! Give us all good whether we ask it or not, and avert from us all evil, tho' we do not pray thee to do so. Bless all our good actions and reward them with success and happiness!'

The envious and sanctimonious who taught and controlled at the shrines and temples expressed their dissent of the comments of Socrates, saying: 'Thou art a false teacher, a corrupter of youth,' and abruptly left the Lyceum.

Then the youthful students, full of admiration, press't forward to grasp his hand, and to praise and thank Plato for his rendition of the poem.

The ladies smiled graciously upon him; some in the midst of the story shed tears, others courtesied low, and all from the Lyceum departed, to sleep and dream of Orpheus and Eurydice.

JOHN PENNIE, JR.

Albany, N. Y.

NOTE.— The doctrine of the Immortality of the soul is fully given by Plato in the Phaedo. A dialogue that contains a philosophic discussion, with a graphic narrative of the last hours of Socrates and his friends, that in pathos and unaffected dignity surpass any other human composition extant.

PAN-AMERICAN EXPOSITION, BUFFALO, N. Y.

Photographed from top of U. S. building.   Olympic grounds.

(By Art Department, New York Tribune.)